GRADES 5-6

...the Super Source®

Geoboards

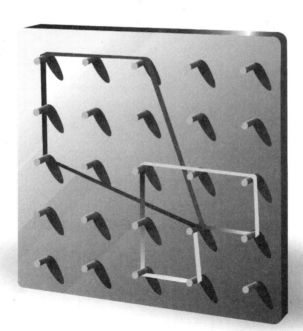

ETA/Cuisenaire®
Vernon Hills, IL

ETA/Cuisenaire® extends its warmest thanks to the many teachers and students across the country who helped ensure the success of the Super Source® series by participating in the outlining, writing, and field testing of the materials.

Project Director: Judith Adams
Managing Editor: Doris Hirschhorn
Editorial Team: John Nelson, Deborah J. Slade, Harriet Slonim, Linda Dodge, Patricia Kijak Anderson
Editorial Assistant: Kerry Heyburn
Field Test Coordinator: Laurie Verdeschi

Design Manager: Phyllis Aycock
Text Design: Amy Berger, Tracey Munz
Line Art and Production: Joan Lee, Fiona Santoianni
Cover Design: Michael Muldoon
Illustrations: June Otani

the Super Source® Geoboards Grades 5–6
ISBN 1-57452-008-3
ETA 015134

ETA/Cuisenaire • Vernon Hills, IL 60061-1862
800-445-5985 • www.etacuisenaire.com

Printed in the United States of America.
03 04 05 06 07 08 09 10 11 12   13 12 11 10 9 8 7 6 5 4

...the Super Source®
Table of Contents

Using the Super Source®

The Super Source® is a series of books, each of which contains a collection of activities to use with a specific math manipulative. Driving **the Super Source** is ETA/Cuisenaire's conviction that children construct their own understandings through rich, hands-on, mathematical experiences. Although the activities in each book are written for a specific grade range, they all connect to the core of mathematics learning that is important to every K–6 child. Thus, the material in many activities can easily be refocused for children in other grade levels. Because the activities are not arranged sequentially, children can work on any activity at any time.

The lessons in **the Super Source** all follow a basic structure consistent with the vision of mathematics teaching described in the *Curriculum and Evaluation Standards for School Mathematics* published by the National Council of Teachers of Mathematics.

All of the activities in this series involve Problem Solving, Communication, Reasoning, and Mathematical Connections—the first four NCTM Standards. Each activity also focuses on one or more of the following curriculum strands: Number, Geometry, Measurement, Patterns/Functions, Probability/Statistics, and Logic.

HOW LESSONS ARE ORGANIZED

At the beginning of each lesson, you will find, to the right of the title, both the major curriculum strands to which the lesson relates and the particular topics that children will work with. Each lesson has three main sections. The first, GETTING READY, offers an *Overview*, which states what children will be doing, and why, and a list of "What You'll Need." Blackline masters that are provided for your convenience at the back of the book are referenced on this list. Paper, pencils, scissors, tape, and materials for making charts, which are necessary in practically every activity, are not.

Although the overhead Geoboard and overhead geodot recording paper are always listed in "What You'll Need" as optional, these materials are highly effective when you want children to see a demonstration on the Geoboard. As you move rubber bands on the screen, children can work with the same materials at their seats. Children can also use the overhead to present their work to other members of their group or to the class.

The second section, THE ACTIVITY, first presents a possible scenario for *Introducing* the children to the activity. The aim of this brief introduction is to help you give children the tools they will need to investigate independently. However, care has been taken to avoid undercutting the activity itself. Since these investigations are designed to enable children to increase their own mathematical power, the idea is to set the stage but not steal the show! The heart of the lesson, *On Their Own*, is found in a box at the top of the second page of each lesson. Here, rich problems stimulate many different problem-solving approaches and lead to a variety of solutions. These hands-on explorations have the potential for bringing children to new mathematical ideas and deepening skills.

On Their Own is intended as a stand-alone activity for children to explore with a partner or in a small group. Be sure to make the directions they need clearly visible. You may want to write them on the chalkboard or on an overhead or to present them on reusable cards or consumable paper. For children who may have difficulty reading the directions, you can read them aloud or make sure that at least one child in each group is "reading."

The last part of this second section, *The Bigger Picture*, gives suggestions for how children can share their work and their thinking and make mathematical connections. Class charts and children's recorded work provide a springboard for discussion. Under "Thinking and Sharing," there are several prompts that you can use to promote discussion. Children will not be able to respond to these prompts with one-word answers. Instead, the prompts encourage children to describe what they notice, tell how they found their results, and give the reasoning behind their answers. Thus children learn to verify their own results, rather than relying on the teacher to determine if an answer is "right" or "wrong." Though the class discussion might immediately follow the investigation, it is important not to cut the activity short by having a class discussion too soon.

The Bigger Picture often includes a suggestion for a "Writing" (or drawing) assignment. These are meant to help children process what they have just been doing. You might want to use these ideas as a focus for daily or weekly entries in a math journal that each child keeps.

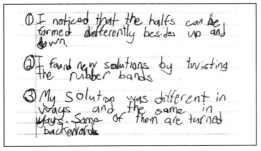

From: *Halving the Geoboard*   **From: *How Many Line Segments?***

The Bigger Picture always ends with ideas for "Extending the Activity." Extensions take the essence of the main activity and either alter or extend its parameters. These activities are well used with a class that becomes deeply involved in the primary activity or for children who finish before the others. In any case, it is probably a good idea to expose the entire class to the possibility of, and the results from, such extensions.

The third and final section of the lesson is TEACHER TALK. Here, in *Where's the Mathematics?*, you can gain insight into the underlying mathematics of the activity and discover some of the strategies children are apt to use as they work. Solutions are also given—when such are necessary and/or helpful. Because *Where's the Mathematics?* provides a view of what may happen in the lesson as well as the underlying mathematical potential that may grow out of it, you want to read the section before presenting the activity to children.

USING THE ACTIVITIES

The Super Source® has been designed to fit into the variety of classroom environments in which it will be used. These range from a completely manipulative-based classroom to one in which manipulatives are just beginning to play a part. You may choose to use some activities in *the Super Source* in the way set forth in each lesson (introducing an activity to the whole class, then breaking the class into groups that all work on the same task, and so forth). You will then be able to circulate among the groups as they work to observe and perhaps comment on each child's work. This approach requires a full classroom set of materials but allows you to concentrate on the variety of ways that children respond to a given activity.

Alternatively, you may wish to make two or three related activities available to different groups of children at the same time. You may even wish to use different manipulatives to explore the same mathematical concept. (Pattern Blocks and Tangrams, for example, can be used to teach some of the same geometric principles as Geoboards.) This approach does not require full classroom sets of a particular manipulative. It also permits greater adaptation of materials to individual children's needs and/or preferences.

If children are comfortable working independently, you might want to set up a "menu"— that is, set out a number of related activities from which children can choose. Children should be encouraged to write about their experiences with these independent activities.

However you choose to use *the Super Source* activities, it would be wise to make time to gather groups or the entire class to share their experiences. The dynamics of this type of interaction, where children share not only solutions and strategies, but also feelings and intuitions, is the basis of continued mathematical growth. It allows children who are beginning to form a mathematical structure to clarify it and those who have mastered just isolated concepts to begin to see how these concepts might fit together.

Again, both the individual teaching style and combined learning styles of the class should dictate the specific method of utilizing *the Super Source* lessons. At first sight, some activities may appear too difficult for some of your children, and you may find yourself tempted to actually "teach" by modeling exactly how an activity can lead to a particular learning outcome. If you do this, you rob children of the chance to try the activity in whatever way they can. As long as children have a way to begin an investigation, give them time and opportunity to see it through. Instead of making assumptions about what children will or won't do, watch and listen. The excitement and challenge of the activity—as well as the chance to work cooperatively—may bring out abilities in children that will surprise you.

If you are convinced, however, that an activity does not suit your students, adjust it, by all means. You may want to change the language, either by simplifying it or by referring to specific vocabulary that you and your children already use and are comfortable with. On the other hand, if you suspect that an activity isn't challenging enough, you may want to read through the activity extensions for a variation that you can give children instead.

RECORDING

Although the direct process of working on the Geoboard is a valuable one, it is afterward, when children look at, compare, share, and think about their constructions, that an activity yields its greatest rewards. However, because Geoboard constructions can't be left intact for very long, children need an effective way to record their work. To this end, various kinds of geodot recording paper are provided for reproduction at the back of this book. The

"What You'll Need" listing at the beginning of each lesson specifies the kind of recording paper to use and what page to find it on. Many teachers have found these to be the most useful for particular activities, but if you find another size to be more appropriate for your class, by all means let your judgment prevail.

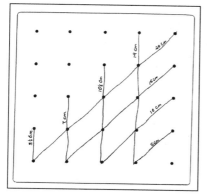

From: *How Many Line Segments?*

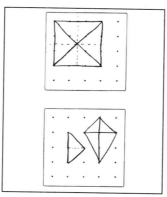

From: *Finding Shapes with Symmetry*

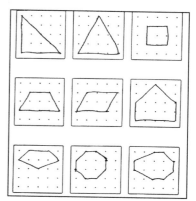

From: *Constructing Polygons*

Paper on which the dots are spaced like the pegs on an actual Geoboard is essential for younger children, who will find recording on paper quite a challenge. Even using same-size paper can frustrate some children.

To help certain children to develop the necessary perceptual skills, you might first have them record by copying from one Geoboard to another. If the original board is the transparent one used on an overhead projector, children can verify that their copies are "the same as," or congruent to, the original by placing the original on top of their work.

Older children can start by using same-size paper but should soon be able to record their constructions on smaller-dot paper. Same-size paper will, however, be extremely useful for work that is to be posted and viewed from a distance.

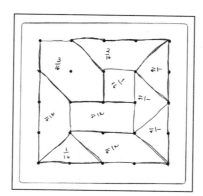

From: *Forming Fractions*

Encourage children for whom recording is a new experience to talk about how they are deciding on the points to connect as they copy their designs. Most children intuitively develop some sort of system for identifying points—for example, children might say, "two pegs up, and one peg over."

Recording involves more than copying constructions. Writing, drawing, and making charts and tables are also ways to record. By creating a table of data gathered in the course of their investigations, children are able to draw conclusions and look for patterns. When children write or draw, either in their group or later by themselves, they are clarifying their understanding of their recent mathematical experience.

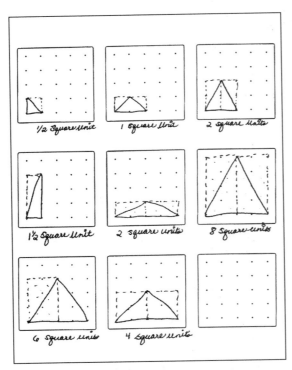

From: Triangle Search

1. Path	Tally	Frequency
AB	I	1
AC	I	1
AD	I	1
AE	I	1
AF	I	1
AG	II	2
AH	III	3
AI	IIII	4
AJ	IIII	5
AK	I	1
AL	III	3
AM	IIII I	6
AN	IIII IIII	10
AO	IIII IIII IIII	15
AP	I	1
AQ	IIII	4
AR	IIII IIII	10
AS	IIII IIII IIII IIII	20
AT	IIII IIII IIII IIII IIII IIII IIII	35
AU	I	1
AV	IIII	5
AW	IIII IIII IIII	15
AX	IIII IIII IIII IIII IIII IIII IIII	35
AY	70	70

2. I used different colors for different pegs.
3. I am sure. I used different colors for different paths.
4. I didn't see any patterns
5. I I did. I just plused the two numbers on the peg letter. I all ones and A,B,C,D,E,F,K,P, and U because I know that there is only one way to get to them.
6. The ones hardest to perdict were the one in the middle because there are a lot of ways to get to them. The ones easiest of predict were the ones on the left side and on the top because to get to the pegs you can only go up and right.
7. Every four letter is a one.

From: How Many Paths?

With a roomful of children busily engaged in their investigations, it is not easy for a teacher to keep track of how individual children are working. Having tangible material to gather and examine when the time is right will help you to keep in close touch with each child's learning.

Exploring Geoboards

A one-sided Geoboard is a sturdy square board with pegs in a square array; a two-sided Geoboard has pegs on both sides, in a square array on one side and in a circular array on the other. The square array consists of 25 pegs evenly spaced in 5 rows of 5 pegs each. The circular array consists of 17 pegs: 12 pegs evenly spaced around the circumference of a circle, 1 peg at the center of the circle, and 1 peg at each corner of the board.

Geoboards are used with multicolored rubber bands. Before children explore on the Geoboard, you may want to show them how to work with the rubber bands. Have children watch as you make a simple shape: Keep a finger on top of a peg to which the rubber band has been secured while you move the rubber band onto and then off a different peg. This technique, which children actually pick up for themselves very quickly, minimizes the chances of rubber bands flying off the board.

By simply stretching rubber bands from peg to peg, children can create all kinds of shapes and designs. This satisfying process encourages children to generate a good deal of work, create variations, and try different solutions without fear of being wrong and without needing to erase their work. Rubber-band constructions fall into place as if by magic, making pleasing patterns with a degree of precision that would otherwise be difficult for children to achieve.

Children need ample time to experiment freely with Geoboards before they begin more serious investigations. Young children enjoy creating pictures, letters, numerals, or simple designs on their Geoboards. Older children are likely to create more involved pictures and designs and make complex—even overlapping—geometric figures.

The rich mathematical structure of the Geoboard enables children to discover mathematical properties with little or no direction from you. They soon notice that a rubber band stretched between two pegs automatically fits into a straight line. (Children may be interested to learn that the word "straight" originated from the Middle English word for "stretched"!) By making line segments, children observe that some pairs of pegs are farther apart than others. They see that by putting a rubber band around a peg and pulling it in two directions, they create a corner (or angle). These and other possibilities for discovery are there for children to mine. Depending on the figures that children create, you may want to bring up certain terminology, but there should be no rush to formalize what is an early process of discovery. Later, when children become involved in the activities, you will find natural occasions to give children the language that can help them to communicate mathematically.

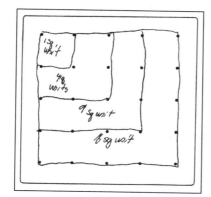

Squar Search

You can make 4 different size shapes.

The area of each squar unit is 1, 4, 9, and 16.

I found all the possible squares because my first one is four and my last is 16 dots and the rest are in between that.

From: *Square Search*

Children often "see" more perfect figures than those they have actually constructed. For example, they may believe that the rubber band around the outer pegs of the circular Geoboard forms a circle, although, in fact, it does not. This ability to automatically overcome a limitation of the Geoboard can facilitate learning. You might still, however, make a point of explaining to children that the unavoidable loop created when the rubber band goes around two pegs should be considered a single line (or segment), even though it may not look like one.

WORKING WITH THE GEOBOARD

The Geoboard is an excellent tool for investigating properties of polygons, congruence, symmetry, angles, area and perimeter, patterns, fractions, coordinate graphing, irrational numbers, and lengths of line segments.

During class discussion, children—especially those in the primary grades—often refer to Geoboard line segments as lines. This may be the time to mention to children that the figures that they form on a Geoboard are really composed of line segments—parts of lines that have a beginning and an endpoint. While it is desirable for children to come to understand the concepts of lines and line segments, emphasize exact terminology only when your children are receptive to it.

As children work through many of the activities, they are called on to test for congruence of shapes and to find the area of shapes. Here are two techniques that you can model so that children will be equipped to do these things successfully.

1. Often, as children come across new solutions to Geoboard activities, they need to check to see if any of their solutions are congruent to others previously found. Some children can check through visualization alone. Others may check for congruency by cutting out the dot-paper recording of one shape and then turning or flipping it to see if it matches another shape exactly. Checking for congruency gives children informal experience with transformational geometry.

2. Many activities require children to find the area of a shape. Although some children may invent ways of doing so for themselves, other children need to see you model some ways to proceed. Demonstrate how noting the position of the sides of a shape in relation to the Geoboard pegs can help children to decide on one of the following methods to use:

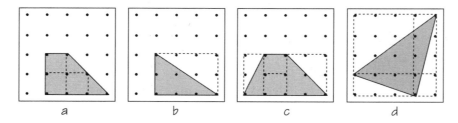

a. Count squares and half squares. (4 square units)
b. Find the area of a right triangle by surrounding it with a rectangle that has twice its area. Then find half the area of that rectangle. (3 square units)
c. Combine methods a and b. (5 square units)
d. Surround the triangle with a square (or rectangle). Find the area of the square and each right triangle. Subtract the total area of the three right triangles from the area of the square. (6.5 square units)

ASSESSING CHILDREN'S UNDERSTANDING

Geoboards are wonderful tools for assessing children's mathematical thinking. Watching children work on their Geoboards gives you a sense of how they approach a mathematical problem. Their thinking can be "seen," in so far as that thinking is expressed through their movement of rubber bands. When a class breaks up into small working groups, you are able to circulate, listen, and raise questions, all the while focusing on how individuals are thinking. Here is a perfect opportunity for authentic assessment.

Having children describe their creations and share their strategies and thinking with the whole class gives you another opportunity for observational assessment. Furthermore, you may want to gather children's recorded work or invite them to choose pieces to add to their math portfolios.

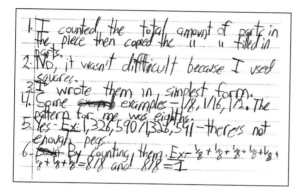

From: *Forming Fractions*

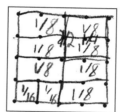
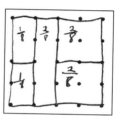

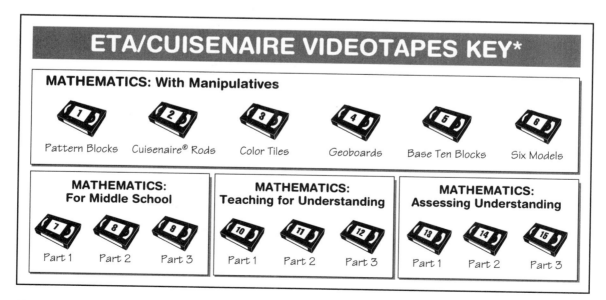

Models of teachers assessing children's understanding can be found in ETA/Cuisenaire's series of videotapes listed below.

ETA/CUISENAIRE VIDEOTAPES KEY*

MATHEMATICS: With Manipulatives

1	2	3	4	5	6
Pattern Blocks	Cuisenaire® Rods	Color Tiles	Geoboards	Base Ten Blocks	Six Models

MATHEMATICS: For Middle School			MATHEMATICS: Teaching for Understanding			MATHEMATICS: Assessing Understanding		
7	8	9	10	11	12	13	14	15
Part 1	Part 2	Part 3	Part 1	Part 2	Part 3	Part 1	Part 2	Part 3

*See *Overview of the Lessons*, pages 16–17, for specific lesson/video correlation.

STRANDS

	PROBLEM SOLVING	COMMUNICATION	REASONING	CONNECTIONS	Geometry	Logic	Measurement	Number	Patterns/Functions	Probability/Statistics
CONSTRUCTING POLYGONS	◆	◆	◆	◆	◆					
COUNT-A-ROUND	◆	◆	◆		◆			◆	◆	
DO YOU GET THE PICTURE?	◆	◆		◆		◆				
FINDING SHAPES WITH SYMMETRY	◆	◆		◆	◆					
FORMING FRACTIONS	◆	◆					◆	◆		
HALVING THE GEOBOARD	◆		◆		◆		◆	◆		
HOW MANY LINE SEGMENTS?	◆	◆			◆		◆			
HOW MANY PATHS?	◆	◆	◆	◆					◆	◆
INSCRIBED TRIANGLES	◆	◆	◆		◆	◆	◆			
MAKING EIGHTHS	◆		◆	◆			◆	◆		
PATTERNS IN AREA	◆	◆	◆	◆	◆		◆		◆	
PEG CAPTURE	◆	◆		◆	◆	◆				
POSSIBLE/IMPOSSIBLE	◆	◆	◆	◆	◆	◆				
SHAPE RIDDLES	◆	◆		◆	◆	◆	◆			
SQUARE SEARCH	◆	◆	◆	◆	◆		◆	◆		
SQUARES AROUND A TRIANGLE	◆	◆	◆		◆		◆		◆	
TRIANGLE SEARCH	◆	◆	◆	◆	◆	◆	◆		◆	
WHAT'S ISOSCELES?	◆	◆	◆	◆	◆		◆		◆	

TOPICS

Angles · Area · Collecting data · Comparing · Congruence · Counting · Equivalent fractions · Fractions · Game strategies · Length · Line segments · Parallel lines · Pattern recognition · Polygons · Properties of geometric figures · Properties of right triangles · Properties of squares · Properties of triangles · Spatial visualization · Symmetry · Transformational geometry · Coordinate geometry

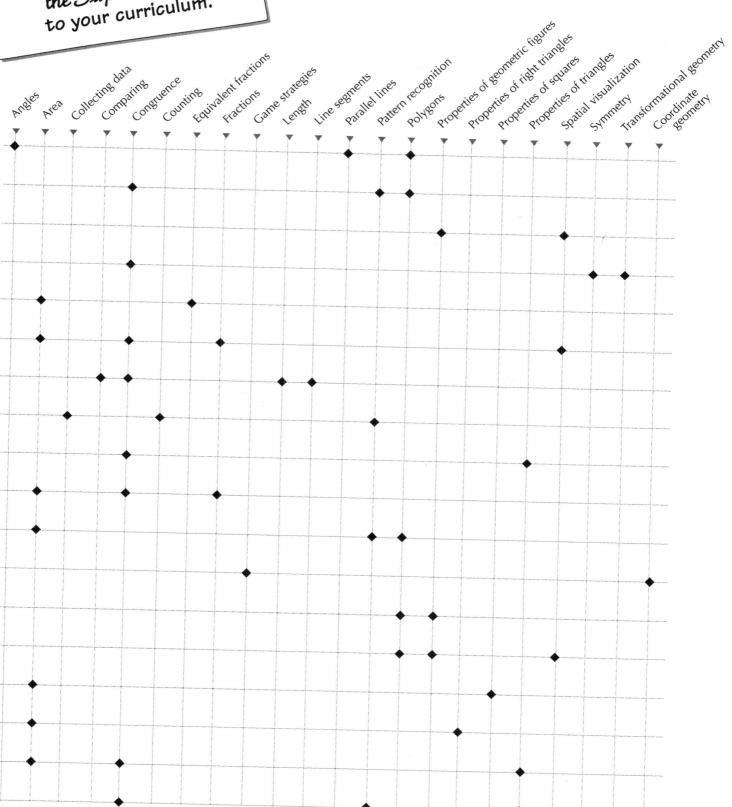

More SUPER SOURCE® at a glance:
GEOBOARDS for Grades K-2 and Grades 3-4

Classroom-tested activities contained in these Super Source® Geoboard books focus on the math strands in the charts below.

the Super Source® Geoboards, Grades K-2

Geometry 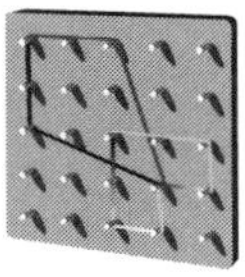	Logic 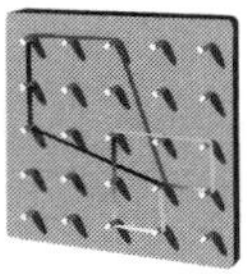	Measurement 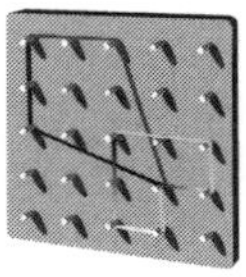
Number 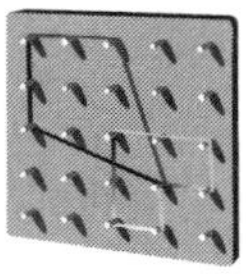	Patterns/Functions 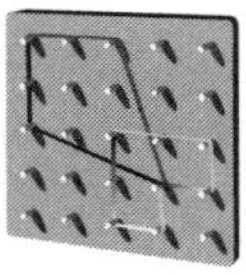	Probability/Statistics 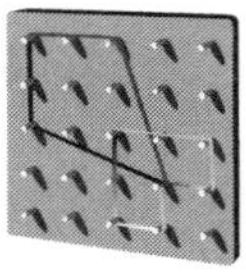

the Super Source® Geoboards, Grades 3-4

Geometry 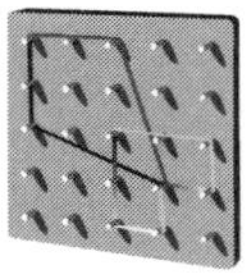	Logic 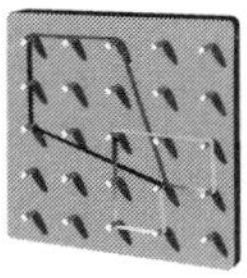	Measurement 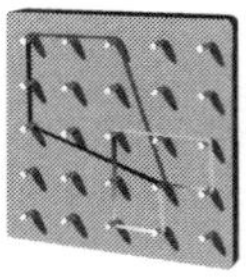
Number	Patterns/Functions	Probability/Statistics

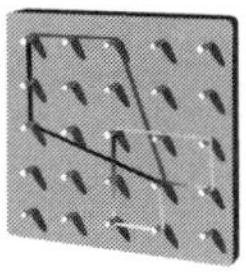

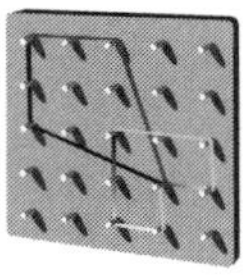

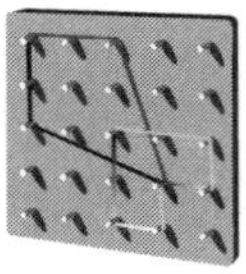

More SUPER SOURCE®
at a glance:
ADDITIONAL MANIPULATIVES
for Grades 5–6

Classroom-tested activities contained in these *Super Source* books focus on the math strands as indicated in these charts.

the Super Source® Base Ten Blocks, Grades 5–6

Geometry	Logic	Measurement
Number	Patterns/Functions	Probability/Statistics

the Super Source® Snap™ Cubes, Grades 5–6

Geometry	Logic	Measurement
Number	Patterns/Functions	Probability/Statistics

the Super Source® Cuisenaire® Rods, Grades 5–6

Geometry	Logic	Measurement
Number	Patterns/Functions	Probability/Statistics

the Super Source® Pattern Blocks, Grades 5–6

Geometry	Logic	Measurement
Number	Patterns/Functions	Probability/Statistics

the Super Source® Color Tiles, Grades 5–6

Geometry	Logic	Measurement
Number	Patterns/Functions	Probability/Statistics

the Super Source® Tangrams, Grades 5–6

Geometry	Logic	Measurement
Number	Patterns/Functions	Probability/Statistics

Overview of the Lessons

See video key, page 11.

Geoboards, Grades 5-6

 See video key, page 11.

CONSTRUCTING POLYGONS

Getting Ready

What You'll Need

Geoboards, 1 per child

Rubber bands

Geodot paper, page 90

Geodot writing paper, page 96

Overhead Geoboard and/or geodot paper transparency (optional)

Overview

Children use their Geoboards to make polygons that meet given sets of conditions. Then they analyze their results. In this activity, children have the opportunity to:

- reinforce their understanding of polygons
- learn about different kinds of polygons
- classify polygons

The Activity

Before children begin the On Their Own *you may want to list some possible attributes of polygons (parallel lines, acute angles, right angles) and talk about each one.*

Introducing

- Establish that a polygon is a closed shape with straight sides, space inside, and no crossing lines.
- Ask children to make a polygon with the fewest sides possible.
- Have children share their polygons with the class and describe them.

On Their Own

> ## Can you make a Geoboard polygon that fits a particular description?
>
> - With a group, make a polygon on your Geoboard to fit each of the descriptions given below. Record your solutions on geodot paper.
>
>   - a 3-sided polygon with as many right angles as possible
>   - a 3-sided polygon with no right angles
>   - a 4-sided polygon with 4 right angles
>   - a 4-sided polygon with only 1 pair of parallel sides
>   - a 4-sided polygon with no right angles, but with 2 pairs of parallel sides
>   - a 5-sided polygon with only 1 pair of parallel sides
>   - a 5-sided polygon with no parallel sides
>   - a 6-sided polygon with 3 pairs of parallel sides
>   - a 6-sided polygon with fewer than 3 pairs of parallel sides
>
> - Think of some ways to sort your solutions.
> - Be ready to discuss your observations and discoveries.

The Bigger Picture

Thinking and Sharing

Have groups take turns sharing their solutions and posting them until there are samples of each of the descriptions listed.

Use prompts like these to promote class discussion:

- What did you discover about polygons, their sides, and their angles?
- What are some ways you could classify your polygons?
- How can you sort the 3-sided polygons, or triangles?
- How can you sort the 4-sided polygons, or quadrilaterals?
- What did you find out about shapes that look the same but are different sizes?
- For which descriptions could you make polygons in which all sides were the same length, or congruent? For which ones is that impossible? Why?
- What do you notice about the posted shapes?

Writing

Have children choose one of the polygons they made and describe how they made it.

Extending the Activity

1. Have children work with partners to write their own polygon description problems. Then have them exchange descriptions with other partners and try to make polygons to fit their descriptions.

Where's the Mathematics?

Children make many observations as they construct polygons on the Geoboard. One of the first things they may notice is that there are multiple solutions to most of the descriptions on the list. Sometimes their solutions may look alike, differing only in size. This can provide one opportunity to explain that polygons that have exactly the same shape but different sizes are said to be *similar* (corresponding angles are congruent and corresponding sides are in proportion). Children may have a basic understanding of similarity as shapes that are enlargements or reductions of one another.

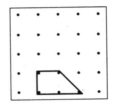 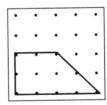

Children may find shapes that are congruent, or exactly the same in both shape and size, but that are simply oriented differently on the Geoboard. By turning the Geoboard or geodot paper they can see that these are not different solutions.

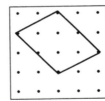 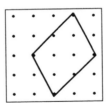

Children may classify their polygons by the number of sides they have. Discuss with children the prefixes, indicating number, in the names of the different shapes—*triangle* (three sides), *quadrilateral* (four sides), *pentagon* (five sides), *hexagon* (six sides), *octagon* (eight sides), *nonagon* (nine sides), *decagon* (ten sides), and so on.

2. Have children make sets of polygons on their Geoboards and use them to play "What's My Rule?" In this game, one child decides on a rule such as "no right angles" or "one pair of parallel sides." He or she then puts the Geoboards into two groups—ones showing shapes that follow the rule and ones showing shapes that don't. The other children in the group then try to guess the rule.

Within each of the groups of polygons, further classifications can be made. For example, a right triangle is a triangle with a right angle. Then there are also different kinds of right triangles: those with two equal sides *(isosceles right triangles)* and those with no equal sides *(scalene right triangles)*. Looking at angles rather than at sides, children may classify triangles into these categories: *right triangles*, triangles with only acute angles *(acute triangles)*, and triangles with one obtuse angle *(obtuse triangles)*.

Children may decide to sort their quadrilaterals according to the number of pairs of parallel sides they have: none, one (trapezoids), or two (parallelograms). They may also sort these groups further, based on lengths of sides and sizes of angles.

Two special quadrilaterals, rhombuses and squares, are interesting for children to investigate, as they are the only *regular polygons* (polygons with congruent sides and congruent angles) that can be made on the Geoboard.

Some of the five- and six-sided shapes that they might make may look very different from the regular pentagons and hexagons children are accustomed to seeing. Children should realize, though, that any shape with five sides is a pentagon, and any shape with six sides is a hexagon. Children might classify their pentagons and hexagons according to those that are *concave* shapes (some vertices pointed inward) and those that are *convex* (all vertices pointed outward).

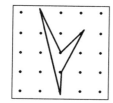

Concave Pentagon
with no parallel sides

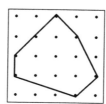

Convex Hexagon
with one pair of parallel sides

COUNT-A-ROUND

- Polygons
- Congruence
- Pattern recognition

Getting Ready

What You'll Need

Geoboards, 1 per child

Rubber bands

Circular geodot paper, pages 93-94

Overhead circular Geoboard and/or circular geodot paper transparency (optional)

Overview

Children count by ones, twos, threes, and so on up to elevens, to select pegs on the circular Geoboard. Then for each of the counting patterns, they connect the corresponding pegs to make shapes. In this activity, children have the opportunity to:

- ◆ make and identify a variety of polygons
- ◆ look for patterns and describe them mathematically
- ◆ discover relationships between numerical and spatial patterns

The Activity

Introducing

- ◆ Ask children to pretend that the circular Geoboard is a clock. Tell them that you are going to use the clock to count off numbers and that the 12 will be the starting peg.

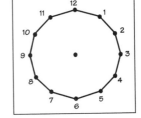

Counting off by 1s

- ◆ Have children work along with you as you count off pegs by 1s. Begin by looping a rubber band around the starting peg and the 1 peg. Then loop another rubber band around the 1 peg and the 2 peg. Continue counting off by 1s until you return to the starting peg.

- ◆ Have children use circular geodot paper to record the 12-sided polygon (dodecagon) that has been formed. Tell them to label it "Counting off by 1s."

On Their Own

What shapes can you make by counting off pegs around your circular Geoboard and connecting them?

- Work with a partner. Use the topmost peg on your circular Geoboard as the starting peg. Create a shape by using rubber bands to connect the pegs in a counting pattern. Here's how to start making a shape by "counting off" by 5s.

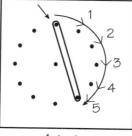 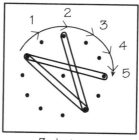

| 1st step | 2nd step | 3rd step |

- Keep counting off by 5s and connecting the pegs. Stop only when you get back to the starting peg, even if that means you have to go around the board more than once.

- Record the shape on circular geodot paper and label it "Counting Off by 5s."

- Create and record more shapes by counting off pegs by 1s, 2s, 3s, 4s, and so on up through 11s.

- Look for a pattern in your solutions.

The Bigger Picture

Thinking and Sharing

Ask volunteers to display a recorded shape for each counting pattern. Post them in order from "Counting off by 1s" through "Counting off by 11s." If there is disagreement about any shape, work together to create that shape on a circular Geoboard.

Use prompts like these to promote class discussion:

- How can you describe the shapes you made using the counting patterns?
- Did some of the shapes surprise you? Explain.
- Are any of the shapes exactly the same size and shape, or congruent? How can you be sure they are congruent?
- What do you notice about the sides of some of the shapes?
- What overall pattern do you see?
- Why do certain counting patterns produce the same shape?

Writing

Ask children to explain how it was possible to produce the same shape using different counting patterns.

Where's the Mathematics?

By using each counting pattern and connecting the resulting pegs on the circular Geoboard, children find that they can make six different designs.

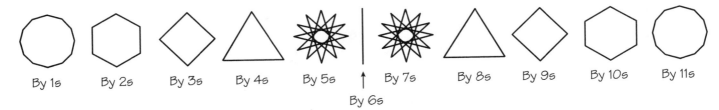

| By 1s | By 2s | By 3s | By 4s | By 5s | ↑
By 6s | By 7s | By 8s | By 9s | By 10s | By 11s |

When children see the designs from the eleven counting patterns displayed in order, they may realize that the overall pattern is symmetrical. For example, with the straight line resulting from counting by 6s as the center, moving out to 5s and 7s they see the 12-pointed star, then moving out to 4s and 8s they see identical triangles, and so on. If children notice this as they are working, it may cause them to question and correct any shape they make that does not fit the pattern.

Children may find it interesting to see that each of the designs except the line segment is repeated. The five designs that were produced by counting off by 1s, 2s, 3s, 4s, and 5s, were also produced by counting off by 11s, 10s, 9s, 8s, and 7s, respectively. However, the number of times that children needed to count around the board—and thus the number of pegs they counted—was different in each of the cases.

Count off by	Times around the Geoboard	Total number of pegs counted
1	1	12
2	1	12
3	1	12
4	1	12
5	5	60
7	7	84
8	2	24
9	3	36
10	5	60
11	11	132

Extending the Activity

Have children investigate what would happen if there were 24 pegs on the circular Geoboard instead of 12. Encourage them to make a prediction first. Then have them use circular geodot paper for the exploration, creating the extra pegs by drawing new dots between the existing dots. Children will find a pattern similar to that formed with the 12 pegs.

Some children may even notice that although two counting patterns produce the same designs, the method of constructing the design for each of these counting patterns is different.

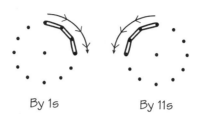

By 1s   By 11s

Since each polygon produced by one of the counting patterns has all equal sides and all equal angles, children may be ready for the term *regular polygon*. An interesting pattern occurs when counting off and creating these regular polygons. The number by which children are counting off divides evenly into the total number of pegs used (12, or a multiple of 12), and the resulting number is the polygon's number of sides and angles. For example:

$12 \div 1 = 12$ Counting off by 1s produces a regular 12-sided figure, or dodecagon

$12 \div 2 = 6$ Counting off by 2s produces a regular 6-sided figure, or hexagon.

$12 \div 3 = 4$ Counting off by 3s produces a regular 4-sided figure, or square.

$12 \div 4 = 3$ Counting off by 4s produces a regular 3-sided figure, or equilateral triangle.

$24 \div 8 = 3$ Counting off by 8s produces a regular 3-sided figure, or equilateral triangle.

$36 \div 9 = 4$ Counting off by 9s produces a regular 4-sided figure, or square.

$60 \div 10 = 6$ Counting off by 10s produces a regular 6-sided figure, or hexagon.

$132 \div 11 = 12$ Counting off by 11s produces a regular 12-sided figure, or dodecagon

Although at this point children may not be able to discover why certain numbers produce certain shapes, they begin to realize that there is a relationship between the numbers by which they count and the shapes that result. This understanding initiates them for further work with patterns and functions in mathematics.

DO YOU GET THE PICTURE?

- Properties of geometric figures
- Spatial visualization

Getting Ready

What You'll Need

Geoboard, 1 per child

Rubber bands

Folders or books to use as a screen to hide Geoboard

Overhead Geoboard and/or geodot paper transparency (optional)

Overview

Children create designs on their Geoboards and describe the designs so that other children can recreate the designs without seeing them. In this activity, children have the opportunity to:

- use geometric language in context
- review and expand their mathematical vocabulary
- prepare and follow a set of directions

The Activity

Introducing

- Show children this Geoboard design.
- Ask them to brainstorm a list of clues about the design that could be used to help someone make the design without actually seeing it. Write the clues on the chalkboard.
- Discuss which clues would be most helpful and which could be confusing and why.
- Have volunteers select a set of clues from the list that would give just enough information.

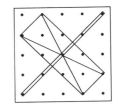

On Their Own

Can you describe a Geoboard design so that someone else will be able to "get the picture"?

- Work in a group. Take turns being the designer. The designer creates a Geoboard design using 3 to 6 rubber bands, but keeps the design hidden from the others in the group.

- The designer describes the design to the group. Each of the other group members tries to build an exact copy, keeping their work hidden from the designer and from each other.

- When the designer feels that the description is complete, he or she asks the others if they've, "got the picture." If everyone says "yes," they all show their designs. If anyone says "no," the designer gives more clues and repeats or clarifies the clues given previously, until everyone has got the picture.

- Compare designs for similarities and differences. Review and discuss the clues. Decide if additional information would have been helpful.

- Continue until every member of the group has had a chance to be the designer.

The Bigger Picture

Thinking and Sharing

Ask each group to discuss any difficulties or insights they had while doing the activity.

Use prompts like these to promote class discussion:

- Which did you prefer: creating a design and its description or recreating someone else's design? Why?

- What kinds of clues were most helpful?

- Were any clues confusing? What were they?

- Which sorts of things did you need to clarify as you went along?

- Did you learn any new vocabulary or review any terms that you had forgotten? Explain.

Writing

Show children a Geoboard with a design on it. Ask them to write a description of the design using the fewest number of clues.

Extending the Activity

1. Ask children to repeat this activity using the circular side of the Geoboard.

2. Have the class create a set of task cards. On one side of the card, have them draw a design on geodot paper. On the other side of the card, have them write the directions for making the design. Then have them exchange cards and try to make the designs.

Teacher Talk

Where's the Mathematics?

Although this activity may be used at any time in the school year, it will provide a richer experience for children if it is used at the end of a geometry unit. At this time children will have built a more solid vocabulary of geometric terms. One way you will know that they appreciate the power of a rich vocabulary is when you hear a child giving his or her clue as "I made the smallest octagon possible in the lower left-hand corner of the Geoboard," rather than "I made the smallest possible eight-sided polygon."

This activity takes on a personality of its own according to the group of children who are doing it. Some groups will insist that color is important and the design must match right down to the color of the rubber bands. Other groups won't even consider color as a factor and will concentrate only on the shape of the design. Some groups will allow a lot of give-and-take between the group members. For example, when the designer says, "There is a isosceles triangle that has one vertex on the center peg," some groups will allow a group member to pipe up and question, "What's an isosceles triangle?" Other groups won't allow the group members to ask any questions at all. Still other groups will allow questions only after the designer has asked, "Do you want any more clues?"

Most frequently, children describe the shape of one rubber band at a time, layering parts of the design. Some children like to create "real objects," for example a face, and then use a clue such as "the nose is a right triangle which points to the left and is three units tall and one unit wide." Using the word "nose" will imply that the location of the triangle is probably in the middle of the Geoboard and the leg that is 1 unit long is probably the horizontal base. Some children describe their shapes with a clue, such as, "It is an octagon that has only 4 pegs outside." The description of "only four pegs outside" limits the location and size of the octagon to only one possibility. Likewise, a clue, such as "It's an isosceles triangle with only 2 pegs inside it." considerably cuts down on the number of possibilities.

3. Ask children to design a system for identifying the pegs on the Geoboard so that they could easily direct someone to place a rubber band on the Geoboard to make a hexagon. Then ask children to write the set of directions that will accomplish this.

Chances are you will hear holdovers from younger days as children describe a shape as an "upside-down triangle" implying that triangles should always point up and sit firmly on a base. They are still apt to describe a square that balances on its vertex as a "diamond." Many may argue that an equilateral triangle is not an isosceles triangle.

Some groups have been known to use or invent a system of numbering or lettering each peg as the Geoboards in the lessons "Peg Capture" and "How Many Paths?" were labeled. They efficiently refer to the triangle below as having vertices (1, 2), (2, 1), and (3, 2) or vertices L, H, and N, and everyone knows immediately where to put their rubber band. Such efficiency takes some of the fun out of the game but the children derive enjoyment from thinking that they have beat the system.

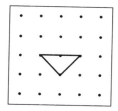 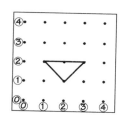 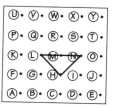

This activity makes a good assessment tool for the teacher. As you listen to the interchange between group members, you will learn which geometric terms or subject areas need further review and which areas seem to be firmly mastered. If you are lucky enough to have a group that labels each point on their Geoboard as described above, you will have a natural introduction to the efficiency of a coordinate graphing system.

FINDING SHAPES WITH SYMMETRY

- Symmetry
- Congruence
- Transformational geometry

Getting Ready

What You'll Need

Geoboards, 1 per child

Rubber bands

Geodot paper, pages 90–91

Overhead Geoboard and/or geodot paper transparency (optional)

Overview

Children use their Geoboards to create designs that have different types of symmetry. In this activity, children have the opportunity to:

- ◆ discover characteristics of symmetrical designs
- ◆ develop strategies that test for symmetry
- ◆ make designs with rotational symmetry and line symmetry

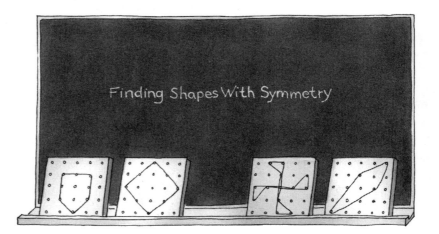

The Activity

Introducing

- ◆ Display this design on your Geoboard. Note the four numbers that correspond to a clockface. Copy the design on geodot paper. Fold it to show that it has horizontal and vertical lines of symmetry.

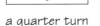

- ◆ Have children make the design on their Geoboards. Ask them to turn the Geoboard design a quarter turn, or 90°, and compare the turned figure to the one on display.

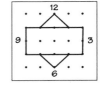

a quarter turn

a half turn

- ◆ Repeat the process for a half turn, or 180°.

- ◆ Elicit that the displayed design looks identical after a half turn, but not after a quarter turn. Therefore, it has half-turn symmetry but not quarter-turn symmetry.

On Their Own

> ### Can you create Geoboard designs with certain kinds of symmetry?
>
> - Work with a partner. Try to create at least 1 design for each of these descriptions:
>   - ◆ The design has at least 1 line of symmetry and looks the same after every quarter turn.
>   - ◆ The design has no lines of symmetry and looks the same after every quarter turn.
>   - ◆ The design has a line of symmetry but no quarter-turn symmetry and no half-turn symmetry.
>   - ◆ The design has quarter-turn symmetry but no half-turn symmetry.
> - Copy your designs onto geodot paper. If you cannot make a design for one of the descriptions, explain why.
> - Be prepared to discuss the different kinds of symmetry in each of your designs.

The Bigger Picture

Thinking and Sharing

Invite children to post some of their designs. Ask volunteers to come up and point out types of symmetry in the various designs. Have children verify that the designs meet the conditions described. If a group believes there are no possible solutions for a part of the problem, have children explain their reasoning.

Use prompts like these to promote class discussion:

- ◆ How did you go about creating your designs?
- ◆ How did you check for lines of symmetry?
- ◆ How did you check for quarter-turn symmetry?
- ◆ How are turn symmetry and line symmetry alike? How are they different?
- ◆ Describe a strategy for creating a design with only one line of symmetry.
- ◆ Describe a strategy for creating a design with quarter-turn symmetry.

Children can use a mirror to see if a shape has lines of symmetry.

Writing

Have children describe how shapes that have symmetry are different from those that do not have symmetry.

Extending the Activity

1. Have children work in pairs. Ask one child in each pair to make a Geoboard design that has quarter-turn symmetry. Then ask the other child to modify the design to create a different design that also has quarter-turn symmetry.

Where's the Mathematics?

Although they may be somewhat familiar with the concept of line symmetry, many children may be unfamiliar with the concept of turn symmetry. To recognize and test for turn symmetry, children may need to turn their Geoboards to see if a rotation of the shape is congruent to the shape in its original orientation. Some children may find it easier to check for turn symmetry by first recording the design in its original orientation on geodot paper and then comparing the rotated Geoboard design to the drawing.

When making designs to fit the first description, children may conclude that any shape that has quarter-turn symmetry must also have line symmetry. The designs they create initially may all have lines of symmetry, reflecting children's previous experiences with symmetric designs. However, in attempting to make a design to fit the second description, some children may come to realize that a shape can have quarter-turn symmetry without also having line symmetry. The examples below show designs that have quarter-turn symmetry, one with line symmetry, and one without.

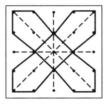

quarter-turn symmetry
4 lines of symmetry

quarter-turn symmetry
no lines of symmetry

To make a design that fits the third description (line symmetry but no turn symmetry), children will need to be sure that the design has only one line of symmetry. Children may find that many simple shapes and letters of the alphabet meet this requirement.

2. Ask each child to make a symmetrical Geoboard design that he or she finds pleasing. Have children copy their designs onto geodot paper and color them to show symmetry.

3. Invite children to create their own Geoboard designs that involve line symmetry and/or turn symmetry. Then ask them to write a description of their designs. Have children exchange descriptions and find designs that fit the descriptions.

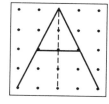

1 line of symmetry
no turn symmetry

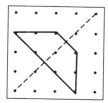

1 line of symmetry
no turn symmetry

As they make shapes and check for turn symmetry, children see that shapes that look the same when turned a quarter of the way around will also look the same when turned halfway around. Based on this experience, children should discover that there is no design that fits the fourth description (quarter-turn symmetry, but no half-turn symmetry).

Children may begin to recognize the characteristics of symmetric designs, but may or may not be able to verbalize their generalizations. Their ability to make successive designs that have certain kinds of symmetry is evidence that they understand the nature of these characteristics.

Working with line and turn symmetry provides children with a foundation for dealing with future studies in transformational geometry, where children will encounter reflections and rotations of geometric shapes in a plane.

FORMING FRACTIONS

• Area
• Equivalent fractions

Getting Ready

What You'll Need

Geoboards, 1 per group

Rubber bands

Geodot paper, pages 90–91

Geodot writing paper, page 96

Overhead Geoboard and/or geodot paper transparency (optional)

Overview

Children divide the Geoboard into regions and find the fractional part of the whole Geoboard represented by each region. In this activity, children have the opportunity to:

◆ find fractional parts of a whole

◆ discover different names for the same fractional part

◆ explore different ways to add fractions

◆ represent fractions spatially

The Activity

You may want to provide some experiences with finding area on the Geoboard before doing this lesson. See introductory material.

Introducing

◆ Show children these Geoboard shapes.

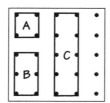 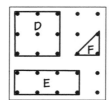 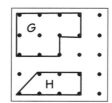

◆ Ask children to tell what fractional part of the Geoboard each shape represents. Encourage them to name as many different fractions as they can for each shape. For example, A = 1/16, B = 2/16 or 1/8, C = 4/16 or 2/8 or 1/4, D = 4/16 or 2/8 or 1/4, E = 3/16, F = 1/32, G = 5/16, and H = 5/32.

◆ Justify the answer by partitioning each of the shapes to show the different, but equivalent fractions.

On Their Own

Can you divide your Geoboard into different-sized regions and find the fractional part represented by each region?

- Work in a group to divide a whole Geoboard into at least 4 regions. Include regions of several different sizes and shapes.

- Use a rubber band to separate each region from the next. No region may be formed by "opening up" a single rubber band as in the second figure. No regions may overlap.

- Find the fractional part of the whole Geoboard that is represented by each region. If you have trouble finding the fractions, make adjustments to the regions on the Geoboard so that the fractions are easier to find.

- Copy the Geoboard regions onto geodot paper. Label each region with the fractional part it represents.

- Find a way to check that all your fractions add up to 1.

The Bigger Picture

Thinking and Sharing

Ask a child from each group to post his or her group's work. Then have children discuss any difficulties or insights they had while doing the activity.

Use prompts like these to promote class discussion:

- How did you decide which fractional name to use for a region?

- What fractional parts were you able to make on your Geoboard? Why?

- What was the most difficult part of the activity? What was the easiest part?

- Did you make any shapes that represented fractions that were hard to find? If so, what did you do?

- Are there some fractions you cannot show on the Geoboard? Explain.

- How did you prove that all your fractions had a sum of one whole?

Drawing and Writing

Have children explain how it is possible for two different fractions to represent the same part of a whole. Ask them to include drawings with their work.

Extending the Activity

1. Have children work in pairs to create fraction puzzles by repeating the activity without labeling the geodot paper drawings. Then have pairs exchange puzzles and figure out the fraction names for each region in each other's designs.

Where's the Mathematics?

In this activity, children work with fractional parts—particularly halves, fourths, eighths, sixteenths, and thirty-secondths—in a geometric setting that involves the concept of area. Since the Geoboard has 16 square units, children see that 8 square units represent the fraction 1/2, 4 square units represent 1/4, 2 square units represent 1/8, 1 square unit represents 1/16, and 1/2 square unit represents 1/32. Depending on the regions children create, these unit fractions may have many different shapes. Some shapes are shown below.

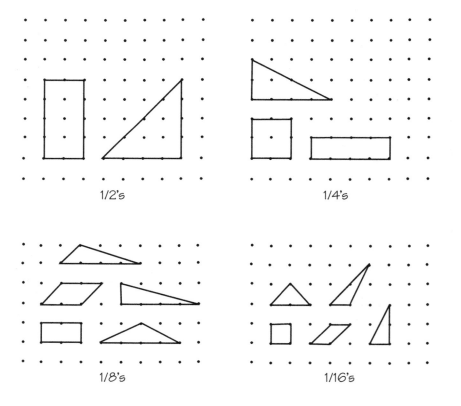

As children find fractions to represent regions, they see that both the shape of a region and how it can be subdivided indicate whether one or several

2. Have children enclose a 3-by-4 rectangle on their Geoboard. Ask them to repeat the activity and then compare the fractions they find with the ones they found on the 4-by-4 square on their Geoboard.

3. Challenge children to repeat the activity without the "no overlapping regions" rule.

---

fractions can be used. For example, the region below can be subdivided into eighths, sixteenths, and thirty-secondths.

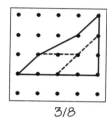
3/8

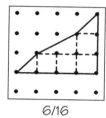
6/16

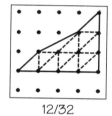
12/32

The region above, 3/8, may be represented by fractions with denominators of 16 and 32, but it cannot be represented by fractions with denominators of 4 or 2. The region to the right, however, can only be represented using thirty-secondths (not by a fraction with 16, 8, 4, or 2 in the denominator). Children may be able to reason that if there are an odd number of units in the area (odd numbers in the numerator as in 3/8 and 5/32), the region cannot be represented by fractions with denominators that are any smaller than they already are.

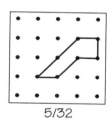
5/32

One way that children may check that their fractions are correct is to add the fractions to see if their sum is 1. To do this, children can express the fraction for each region with the same denominator.

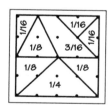

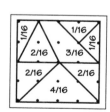

$\frac{1}{16} + \frac{1}{8} + \frac{3}{16} + \frac{1}{16} + \frac{1}{16} + \frac{1}{8} + \frac{1}{4} + \frac{1}{8}$ or $\frac{1}{16} + \frac{2}{16} + \frac{3}{16} + \frac{1}{16} + \frac{1}{16} + \frac{2}{16} + \frac{4}{16} + \frac{2}{16} = 1$

Some children may come up with strategies for adding the fractional parts that involve subdividing, renaming, and/or combining the regions.

HALVING THE GEOBOARD

- Area
- Congruence
- Fractions
- Spatial visualization

Getting Ready

What You'll Need

Geoboards, 1 per child

Rubber bands

Geodot paper, pages 90–91

Overhead Geoboard and/or geodot paper transparency (optional)

Overview

Children search for different ways to divide the Geoboard into halves. In this activity, children have the opportunity to:

◆ discover that halves of the same shape have the same area

◆ recognize that shapes with the same area may not look alike

The Activity

You may want to provide some experiences with finding area on the Geoboard before doing this lesson. See introductory material.

Explain that by flipping or turning the Geoboard the same solution is simply repositioned.

Introducing

- ◆ Ask the children to construct a 4-by-4 square on their Geoboards. Tell them that the rubber band encloses one whole square.
- ◆ Have them use another rubber band to divide the square into halves.
- ◆ Invite several volunteers to show their Geoboards. Ask them to explain what it means to divide a square in half.

On Their Own

How many ways can you divide your Geoboard into halves?

- Work with a partner to construct a 4-by-4 square on a Geoboard. Divide it into halves in at least 10 different ways.

  - Be sure that your solutions are all different, not just flips or turns of each other.

  - Be sure that each of your solutions is made up of only 2 parts.

- Record your solutions on geodot paper.

- Be prepared to explain why your solutions show halves.

Okay
(2 parts)

Not okay
(3 parts)

The Bigger Picture

Thinking and Sharing

Ask a volunteer from each group to post one of the different solutions and explain how it shows halves. Continue until all of the solutions have been posted and everyone agrees that there are no duplicates.

Use prompts like these to promote class discussion:

- What did you notice about the sizes and shapes of halves?

- How did you go about finding new solutions?

- Are any of the solutions the same in some way? Explain.

- What do all the halves have in common?

- Do you think there is any limit to the number of solutions? Explain.

If any solution is disputed, you can have all groups reproduce the solution and work to figure out and compare the areas of the two parts.

Writing

Ask children to write about their strategies for dividing a larger square into halves.

Extending the Activity

1. Have children find different ways to divide the Geoboard into fourths.

2. Have children use a rubber band to enclose 12 or 15 small squares on the Geoboard. Then ask them to find different ways to divide this region into thirds.

Where's the Mathematics?

As children investigate the various ways to divide the Geoboard into halves, they work with the concepts of congruence, area, and fractional parts. Their exploration also prompts children to think of fractions in spatial terms. There are many solutions to the problem, and children will probably not have time to find and prove them all. It is sufficient that they find enough solutions to indicate the great variety of ways the problem can be solved, as well as to recognize that all solutions consist of two regions that have the same area.

Children may start by dividing the Geoboard with one line segment that passes through the center peg and is parallel to a side of the Geoboard. They might then go on to make other segments that pass through the center peg.

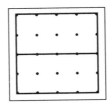   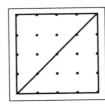   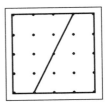

To find other solutions, children will need to realize that the dividing line does not have to be straight. One strategy is to first divide the Geoboard diagonally and then move opposite ends of the rubber band one peg at a time in opposite directions.

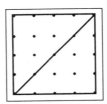   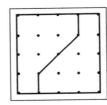   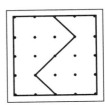

To find other kinds of solutions, children need to realize that the halves do not have to be congruent; it is only necessary that they cover half of the 16 unit squares on the Geoboard.

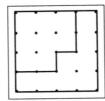   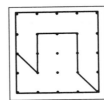

Thus, children begin to realize that for a region to be half of the Geoboard, it must have an area of 8 square units. So children develop strategies for finding the area of each region. One strategy is to partition the shape, determine the area of its parts, and then add these areas together, as shown in A. Another way is to enclose the shape with another figure, such as a rectangle, determine the area of the rectangle, and then subtract the areas of the parts of the rectangle that lie outside the original shape, as shown in B. A combination of these two techniques is shown in C.

Areas of the Shaded Regions

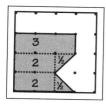

A

Area = 3 + 2 + 2 + ½ + ½
     = 8 square units

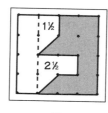

B

Area = 12 − 1½ − 2½
     = 8 square units

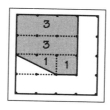

C

Area = 3 + 3 + 1 + 1
     = 8 square units

In searching for as many solutions as possible, children need to use logical reasoning in a geometric context. For example, some children may begin to create new solutions from existing ones by transferring the position of a unit square within the same region.

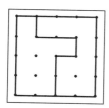

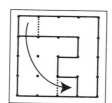

Although children may start their exploration by making halves in random fashion, they often develop a system for searching for other solutions.

HOW MANY LINE SEGMENTS?

Getting Ready

What You'll Need

Geoboards, 1 per child

Rubber bands

Geodot paper, pages 90–91

Geodot writing paper, page 96

Measuring tools (rulers, straws, pipe cleaners, strips of oak tag)

Overhead Geoboard and/or geodot paper transparency (optional)

Overview

Children try to make all the different-length line segments that can be made on the Geoboard. In this activity, children have the opportunity to:

◆ compare lengths of line segments

◆ identify congruent line segments

◆ order line segments by length

The Activity

Point out that the unavoidable rubber band loop is considered a single line segment.

You might explain that a line has no beginning point and no ending point, and that a line segment is part of a line.

Introducing

◆ Make a horizontal line segment 2 units long on your Geoboard and show it to the class. Explain that the figure formed by this rubber band is called a line segment and that a line segment is straight, has no bends, and has a definite beginning and endpoint.

◆ Using the distance between two adjacent vertical or horizontal pegs as the unit of measure, establish that your line segment is 2 units long.

◆ Ask children to make a line segment the same length as yours. Have them hold up their Geoboards for all to see.

◆ Point out that all line segments that have the same length are congruent, regardless of where they are on the Geoboard.

On Their Own

How many different-length line segments can you make on your Geoboard?

- Work with a partner to make line segments of as many different lengths as you can.

- Record your segments on geodot paper.

- Order the segments by length from shortest to longest.

- Be ready to explain how you know you have found line segments for all the possible lengths.

The Bigger Picture

Thinking and Sharing

Have groups share their recordings and the methods they used for comparing and ordering their line segments. If there are disagreements, suggest children check their work by applying a few different comparison strategies. Then call on volunteers to post solutions until the class is satisfied that all solutions are posted.

It may be helpful to allow children to cut around the geodot paper segments so they can compare their lengths.

Use prompts like these to promote class discussion:

- ◆ How did you compare the lengths of different line segments?

- ◆ What is the longest segment you can make on the Geoboard? Explain how you know it is the longest.

- ◆ In order from largest to smallest, which segment is next? How can you be sure of this?

- ◆ What is the shortest segment that can be made? Explain how you know it is the shortest.

- ◆ In order from smallest to largest, which segment is next? How can you be sure of this?

- ◆ How could you prove to someone else that the segments you made show the only lengths that are possible to make on the Geoboard?

Writing

Ask children to explain how they compared and ordered the segments they made.

Extending the Activity

Have children repeat the activity using only a one-by-one unit region of the Geoboard, a two-by-two unit region, and a three-by-three unit region. Have them look for patterns in the number of solutions and predict the number of different-length line segments on a five-by-five unit Geoboard.

Where's the Mathematics?

There are 14 different-length line segments that can be made on the four-by-four unit Geoboard. Of these, the shortest line segment connects two horizontally adjacent or vertically adjacent pegs, and the longest is the diagonal line segment that is formed by connecting pegs in opposite corners of the Geoboard.

Children may begin by creating line segments that run horizontally or vertically across the Geoboard. In comparing the lengths of those line segments, children find that there are only four possible lengths. There are also 10 slanted line segments, each with a unique length.

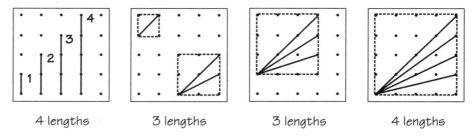

| 4 lengths | 3 lengths | 3 lengths | 4 lengths |

Children may find the slanted line segments by working from a particular peg and then forming all possible non-vertical and non-horizontal line segments. As they compare the lengths of these segments, children realize that some of these segments are congruent, and then work to eliminate any lengths that are repeated.

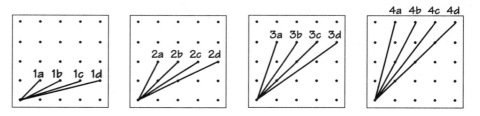

Children can find the congruent line segments without measuring. For example, line segments 1b and 2a are congruent because each is the length of the diagonal of same-sized, or congruent, rectangles.

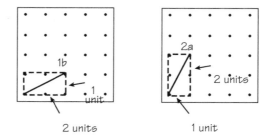

Children can use the same method to find 5 more congruent pairs, thus revealing that there are 10 different-length slanted line segments.

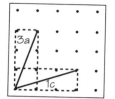
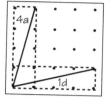
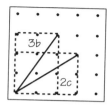

1c is congruent to 3a.   1d is congruent to 4a.   2c is congruent to 3b.

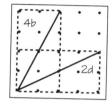
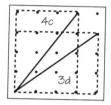

2d is congruent to 4b.   3d is congruent to 4c.

To measure and compare the lengths of their line segments, some children may choose to use a ruler, either to measure the lengths on the Geoboard or to measure drawings of these line segments on geodot paper. In some cases, children may find the difference between lengths to be very slight and difficult to determine with a ruler. Since the task does not require children to identify the actual lengths of the line segments, they may use different kinds of measuring tools, such as oak tag strips, straws, and pipe cleaners, to compare and order lengths.

The order of the segments, from shortest to longest, is:

1, 1a, 2, 1b or 2a, 2b, 3, 1c or 3a, 2c or 3b, 4, 1d or 4a, 3c, 2d or 4b, 3d or 4a, 4d

Children's approaches to completing the task may vary. Some children may search randomly for new line segments, recording them on dot paper as they are found. Some groups of children may split up the task in an attempt to work systematically. Other children may cut out straws or pipe cleaners in lengths that match their line segments, order them, and tape or glue them to a sheet of construction paper. Sharing their strategies helps children to see the variety of approaches and techniques that are possible, and adds to their bank of problem-solving strategies for future activities.

HOW MANY PATHS?

- Counting
- Collecting data
- Pattern recognition

Getting Ready

What You'll Need

Geoboards, 1 per child

Rubber bands

Sticky dots

Geodot paper, page 91

Overhead Geoboard and/or geodot paper transparency (optional)

Overview

Children search for all possible paths that can be made from a corner peg to each of the other pegs on a Geoboard. In this activity, children have the opportunity to:

- ◆ analyze data to find patterns
- ◆ use patterns to make predictions
- ◆ relate visual patterns to numerical patterns
- ◆ investigate counting methods

The Activity

Introducing

- ◆ Before introducing the lesson, use sticky dots to label a Geoboard's pegs from A to Y as shown.
- ◆ Display the Geoboard and ask children to imagine that the Geoboard is the street map of a town in which their house is at peg A, and the school is at peg H. Call on a volunteer to use a rubber band to mark one path from the house to the school. Explain that the path must go along the streets of the town, which run vertically and horizontally, and that it must go only upward and to the right.
- ◆ Call on other volunteers to show different paths from A to H. Elicit that there are three possible paths, and each is 3 units in length.

Show children how they can record the paths using the peg letters:

A B C H
A B G H
A F G H

On Their Own

How many different paths can you find from peg A
to each of the other pegs on your Geoboard?

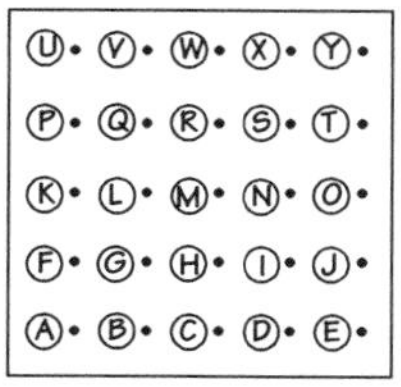

U· V· W· X· Y·
P· Q· R· S· T·
K· L· M· N· O·
F· G· H· I· J·
A· B· C· D· E·

- Work with a group. Put sticky dots on your Geoboard to mark it like a "street map" as shown.

- Find all the paths from A to B, from A to C, from A to D, and so on. Here are the rules for making paths:

  - Paths must go either horizontally or vertically from one peg to the next.
  - Paths may be made only by moving upward or to the right from one peg to the next.

- Keep track of the paths you find. Look for patterns.

- If you can, use your patterns to predict the number of different paths possible without actually finding them on your Geoboard.

The Bigger Picture

Thinking and Sharing

Draw a large Geoboard on the chalkboard or on an overhead geodot transparency. Label the pegs A to Y as shown above. Point to B and ask a volunteer for the number of different paths from A to B. Write this number over B. Repeat this process for every other peg.

Use prompts like these to promote class discussion:

- Did anyone find a different number of paths to any of the pegs? Explain how you found that number.

- How did you keep track of the paths from A to each of the other pegs?

- How were you sure you did not miss or repeat a path?

- Did you notice any patterns while you were working?

- Were you able to predict how many paths there might be to a peg? If so, how were you able to do this?

- For which pegs were the numbers easiest to predict? For which pegs were they more difficult?

- Looking at the entire set of data, what other patterns can you find?

Writing

Ask children to describe how they went about finding all the possible paths.

Extending the Activity

Ask children to imagine they have a Geoboard that has 6 pegs on a side. Have them predict the number of different paths to each new peg. Encourage children to use the number patterns they discovered to help them predict. After children have made their predictions, have them test a few by actually making and counting the paths using geodot paper.

Where's the Mathematics?

There are 24 different pairs of starting pegs and ending pegs (A-B, A-C, A-D,…, A-X, A-Y) and a total of 250 paths. As children work through the activity, they find that it is a challenge to keep track of the many paths they find. Some children may copy each path onto geodot paper as they find it. Other children may try using many different-colored rubber bands and several different Geoboards. Some groups may develop a systematic way of searching for all possible paths to a peg, perhaps splitting up the task among group members.

Children may decide to first investigate all routes in which the first move (or moves) is upward, and then work on those where the first move (or moves) is to the right. Other children may search more randomly, and use some type of recording system. Here is one possible way of recording paths from peg A to each of pegs K, L, and M:

A→K	A→L	A→M
AFK	ABGL	ABCHM
(1 path)	AFGL	ABGHM
	AFKL	ABGLM
	(3 paths)	AFGHM
		AFGLM
		AFKLM
		(6 paths)

Children may have trouble keeping track of the many paths that connect peg A to pegs in the upper right section of the Geoboard. Thus, they may look for helpful patterns. They may also find that patterns help them check the results they have already gathered.

As children record and examine the number of possible paths between pegs, a number of different patterns emerge from their data. If they record the number of paths on geodot paper they may notice that there is only one possible path to each of the pegs in the same row or column that contains peg A. They may also notice that the numbers begin to form a symmetrical pattern.

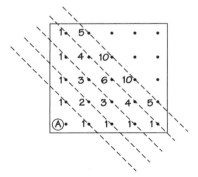

Symmetrical pattern
in numbers of paths from peg A

As they continue to collect the data and record it, some children may discover that the number of paths to a peg is the sum of the number of paths to the pegs immediately to the left of and below it. For example, since there are 4 paths from peg A to peg I and 6 paths from peg A to peg M, there will be 10 paths from peg A to peg N.

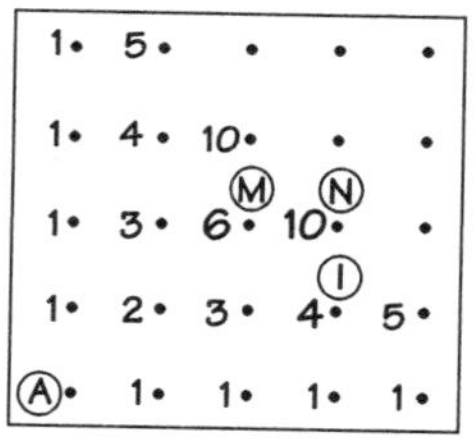

```
1•   5•    •     •     •

1•   4•  10•     •     •

1•   3•   6Ⓜ  10Ⓝ     •

1•   2•   3•   4Ⓘ   5•

Ⓐ•   1•   1•   1•   1•
```

This pattern can be used to find the number of paths to each of the pegs.

```
1•   5•  15•  35•  70•

1•   4•  10•  20•  35•

1•   3•   6•  10•  15•

1•   2•   3•   4•   5•

Ⓐ•   1•   1•   1•
```

Looking at the completed work, children will see part of a pattern known as Pascal's Triangle.

```
              1
            1   1
          1   2   1
        1   3   3   1
      1   4   6   4   1
    1   5  10  10   5   1
  1   6  15  20  15   6   1
```

Pascal's Triangle

Children may be interested in using number patterns to extend the triangle, to see how it continues to develop. The process of seeking out patterns deepens children's sense of the relationships that exist between numbers, crucial to their future success in understanding algebraic concepts.

INSCRIBED TRIANGLES

- **Properties of triangles**
- **Congruence**

Getting Ready

What You'll Need

Circular Geoboard, 1 per child

Rubber bands

Rulers

Circular geodot paper, page 94

Overhead circular Geoboard and/or circular geodot paper transparency (optional)

Overview

Children find all the possible triangles that may be inscribed in a circular Geoboard. They then find the measure of each angle in the inscribed triangles. In this activity, children have the opportunity to:

- use logical reasoning to search for all possibilities
- learn that an inscribed angle measures 1/2 its intercepted arc
- learn that the sum of the measures of the angles of a triangle is 180°

The Activity

Review with children that a circle has 360 degrees.

Inscribed rectangle

Inscribed angle

Introducing

- Show children a circular Geoboard and ask them to imagine that it is a clock. Tell them that one full circle around the clockface represents 360°.
- Use your finger to trace the arc from the 12 peg to the 1 peg. Establish that the arc connecting consecutive pegs is 1/12 of the circle, or 30°.
- Explain that the rectangle at the left on the circular Geoboard is an *inscribed rectangle* because each vertex is at a peg on the circle.
- Moving the rubber band from the 6 peg to the 12 peg forms one right angle. Tell children this is called an *inscribed angle*.
- Show how the sides of this angle cut through at the 2 peg and the 8 peg on the circle. Since the arcs from peg to peg measure 30°, this angle cuts through, or intercepts, an arc of 180°.
- Point out that the number of degrees in an inscribed angle is half the number of degrees in the arc it intercepts.

On Their Own

> ## How many different triangles can be inscribed on a circular Geoboard?
>
> - Work with a partner to create as many different inscribed triangles on your circular Geoboard as you can. Remember that *all 3 vertices of an inscribed triangle must be at pegs on the circle.*
>
>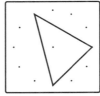
>
> Inscribed triangle   Not an inscribed triangle
>
> - Find the measure of each angle of the triangles you make. Remember that:
>   - Each are from peg to peg around the circle measures 30°.
>   - An inscribed angle has half the number of degrees of the arc of the circle that it cuts through.
>
> - Record each triangle and its angle measurements on circular geodot paper.
> - Organize your data and look for patterns so you are convinced that you have found all of the possible inscribed triangles.

The Bigger Picture

Thinking and Sharing

Ask volunteers, one by one, to create one of the triangles they found on their Geoboard, put the Geoboard on the chalk tray, and write the angle measurements above it. Continue until children feel that every possible triangle is displayed. Discuss their findings.

Use prompts like these to promote class discussion:

- Did you have a plan for solving this problem? What was it?
- What patterns did you notice? Why do you think these patterns exist?
- How were you convinced that you found all of the possible triangles?

Writing

Ask children to explain why the sum of the angles of a triangle has exactly one-half as many degrees as a circle.

Extending the Activity

Ask children to inscribe different polygons, such as quadrilaterals or pentagons, on the Geoboard and measure their angles. Have them describe any patterns they find.

Where's the Mathematics?

This activity introduces children to the power of deductive reasoning. From one fact—an inscribed angle equals half its intercepted arc—they can figure out many more facts. The twelve different inscribed triangles are shown below.

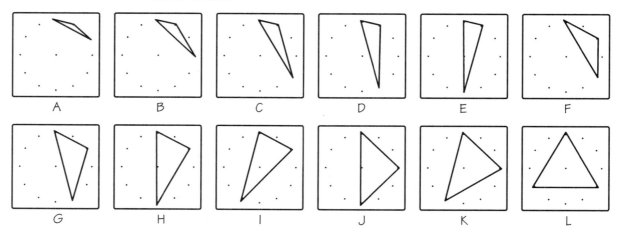

At first, children may think that there are more than 12 triangle solutions because they may have the same triangle redrawn in a different orientation. For example, they may think that these solutions are different. However, checking the angle measurements or rotating the Geoboards until the two triangles are in similar positions should convince them that these are indeed the same triangle.

One of the most powerful patterns that the children may recognize is that the sum of the angles of every triangle is 180°. Even for children who already "knew" this fact, seeing how the 180° of the triangle relates to the 360° of the circle can be a new experience. When asked to explain why this pattern exists, children may point out that the three angles of the triangle taken together intercept the entire circle. For example, in the triangle below, the angle with its vertex at the 12 peg intercepts the arc from 1 to 4; the angle with its vertex on 1 intercepts the arc from 4 to 12; and the third angle intercepts the arc from 12 to 1. These three intercepted arcs put together form the entire 360° circle. Since each inscribed angle is one-half its intercepted arc, the sum of the three angles of the triangle is one-half of 360°, or 180°.

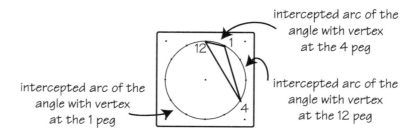

intercepted arc of the angle with vertex at the 4 peg

intercepted arc of the angle with vertex at the 1 peg

intercepted arc of the angle with vertex at the 12 peg

Children may also notice the patterns in the sizes of the angles of the inscribed triangles.

	first angle	second angle	third angle		first angle	second angle	third angle
A	15	15	150	G	30	45	105
B	15	30	135	H	30	60	90
C	15	45	120	I	30	75	75
D	15	60	105	J	45	45	90
E	15	75	90	K	45	60	75
F	30	30	120	L	60	60	60

The measure of each of the angles is a multiple of 15° because 15° is half the measure of the smallest arc that can be formed on a circular Geoboard. Each time the side of an inscribed angle is moved to the next adjacent peg to intercept a larger arc, the size of the inscribed angle increases by 15°. If children list the angles as shown above, starting with all the triangles whose smallest angle is 15°, then all triangles whose smallest angle is 30°, and so forth, they will notice that the second smallest angle increases by 15° while the largest angle decreases by 15°.

Some children may have organized their triangles according to angle size. There are three acute triangles, three right triangles, and six obtuse triangles. Children may notice that all of the right triangles have a diameter of the circle as their longest side. All of the obtuse triangles lie on one side of an imaginary diameter

right triangle

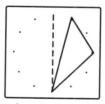
obtuse triangle

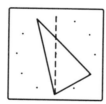
acute triangle

and have an area smaller than the right triangles, whereas the acute triangles cross the imaginary diameter at two points and have an area greater than the right triangles.

Some children will say they were convinced that they had found all possible triangles because they checked their solutions against those of their classmates. Others will explain that they were convinced because they had an organized approach to the problem, such as always keeping one vertex on the 12 peg and then moving the other two vertices in a logical way so they knew that they had hit every peg. Some will point to collecting data and then making an organized table from that data as the method that convinced them that they had found all of the solutions. Sharing these strategies will help students learn new ways to help them approach similar problems with lots of data.

MAKING EIGHTHS

- Area
- Congruence
- Fractions

Getting Ready

What You'll Need

Geoboards, 1 per child

Rubber bands

Geodot paper, pages 90–91

Geodot writing paper, page 96

Overhead Geoboard and/or geodot paper transparency (optional)

Overview

Children explore different ways of dividing the Geoboard into congruent and non-congruent eighths. In this activity, children have the opportunity to:

- ◆ divide a whole into fractional parts
- ◆ represent fractions spatially
- ◆ find the area of a variety of shapes

The Activity

You may want to provide some experiences with finding area on the Geoboard before doing this lesson. See introductory material.

Introducing

- ◆ Have children enclose all 25 pegs on their Geoboard with one rubber band. Explain that this square is to be considered one whole.

- ◆ Ask children to divide their Geoboards into halves that are the same in size and shape, or are congruent. Have them hold up their Geoboards for the other children to see. Have volunteers explain how they know they have divided the square in half.

- ◆ Now ask children to divide their Geoboards into halves that do not have the same shape, or are non-congruent. Discuss ways to prove that these shapes are halves.

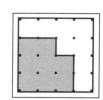

- ◆ Invite children to explain what it would mean to divide the Geoboard into fourths.

On Their Own

How can you divide your Geoboard into eighths?

- Work with a partner. First, try to find different ways to divide your Geoboard into 8 congruent parts (that is, 8 parts with the same size and shape).

- Next, see if you can find different ways to divide your Geoboard into eighths that are noncongruent or don't have the same shape.

- Look for several solutions for each part of the problem.

- Record your solutions on geodot paper.

- Be ready to explain how you know whether your shapes are congruent or noncongruent, and how you can prove that they are eighths.

The Bigger Picture

Thinking and Sharing

Have children share the ways they found for dividing their Geoboards into congruent eighths. If their solutions are very similar, allow time to see if they can come up with additional solutions. Then have them share their solutions for finding noncongruent eighths. One way to do this is to have groups exchange and check each other's divisions. If any problems are noticed, the groups can work together to resolve them.

Use prompts like these to promote class discussion:

- How many different shapes can be used to divide the Geoboard into congruent eighths? How do you know these are the only possibilities?

- What was your strategy for filling the board with noncongruent shapes that were eighths?

- What are some ways to prove that two shapes are either congruent or noncongruent?

- What did you notice about the area of each of the congruent eighths? of each of the noncongruent eighths?

- What did you notice about the perimeters of the eighths you made?

Drawing and Writing

Have children write an explanation of how they went about dividing their Geoboard into noncongruent eighths. Ask them to show the eighths on geodot paper to illustrate their explanation.

Extending the Activity

Ask children to make several shapes that are an eighth of the Geoboard but have different numbers of sides. For example, can they make an eighth that has 3 sides? 4 sides? 5 sides? 6 sides? Ask them to experiment to find the eighth with the largest perimeter.

Where's the Mathematics?

As they explore different ways of dividing the Geoboard into eighths, children work with the concepts of fractions, area, and congruence. They discover that the eighths they make can have different shapes as long as each has an area equal to two small Geoboard squares. Children also discover that there is a great deal of variety in the shapes they can make.

There are four basic shapes children can use to divide the Geoboard into congruent eighths, although these shapes can be arranged in different ways.

CONGRUENT EIGHTHS

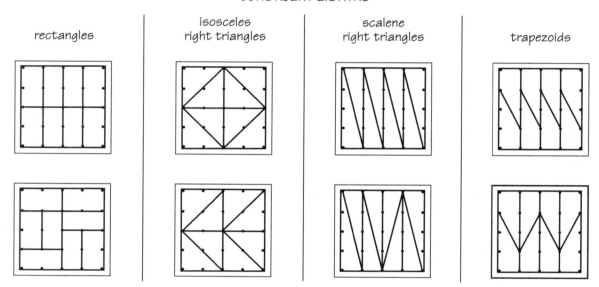

| rectangles | isosceles right triangles | scalene right triangles | trapezoids |

There are many strategies children may use to partition their Geoboard. In searching for congruent eighths, some children may make a shape along the border of the Geoboard, and then try to fill the Geoboard by making seven more of the same shape. Other children may first recognize that one eighth of the Geoboard is 2 square units and then try to fill the Geoboard with congruent shapes that have area of 2 square units. Some children may divide their Geoboards first into congruent halves, and then divide those halves into congruent halves to create congruent fourths, and then divide the fourths into congruent halves to create congruent eighths.

There are many shapes that can be made that are an eighth of the Geoboard, but filling the board with non-congruent eighths means finding eight of these that fit together. This will likely be a challenge for most children. Some may construct their solutions one figure at a time. They may make one shape and check to see if it is one eighth of the Geoboard. Then they may make a different shape, check to see if it is one eighth, and then check to be sure it is not congruent to the previously made shape. Some children may need to reproduce each shape on geodot paper and then flip it or turn it to make sure it is not congruent to shapes already made. Using this one-shape-at-a-time strategy may lead children to partition the Geoboard in ways that leave spaces that are not eighths of the Geoboard. To avoid this, you might suggest that children work along the borders and then inward so they do not cut off space along the border.

Some children may first make, record, and cut out a variety of shapes that each have an area of 2 square units. They then may experiment with the cutouts to look for eight different eighths that fit together. Two examples of Geoboards divided into non-congruent eighths are shown below.

NON-CONGRUENT EIGHTHS

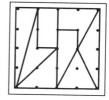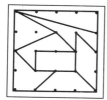

As children search for solutions, they will need to check that their shapes are indeed eighths. In the case where the shapes are   5, children may recognize that the shapes will be eighths if eight of them fill the Geoboard completely. In the case where the shapes are not congruent, children realize that checking for eighths requires finding the area of the shapes they make. Once children learn that eighths must all have the same area, they may think that they also must have the same perimeter. Further exploration will prove that this is not the case, and will provide a context in which children can discover that shapes with the same area may have different perimeters.

PATTERNS IN AREA

Getting Ready

What You'll Need

Geoboards, 1 per child

Rubber bands

Geodot paper, pages 90–91

Overhead Geoboard and/or geodot paper transparency (optional)

Overview

Children make a variety of polygons on their Geoboards, each having a specified number of boundary pegs and interior pegs. They then find the areas of their polygons and search for patterns in the areas. In this activity, children have the opportunity to:

- explore strategies for finding areas of polygons
- collect and organize data
- look for patterns
- use patterns to make predictions and form generalizations

The Activity

You may want to provide some experiences with finding area on the Geoboard before doing this lesson. See introductory material.

Make sure children understand the difference between boundary pegs and interior pegs. This distinction may be clearer to children on geodot paper.

6 boundary pegs, 3 interior pegs

Introducing

- Ask children to make a polygon on their Geoboard that has 4 pegs along its boundary and no pegs in its interior. Explain that not all of the boundary pegs need to be corners, or vertices, of the shape.

- Have children hold up their Geoboards. Point out the variety of possible shapes.

- Ask children to find the areas of their polygons.

- Have them share their results.

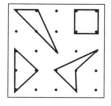

4 boundary pegs, 0 interior pegs
Each area is 1 sq. unit.

On Their Own

How is the area of a Geoboard polygon related to its boundary pegs and interior pegs?

- Work in a group. First explore all the possible areas of polygons that have 3 boundary pegs. Do this by investigating polygons that have 3 boundary pegs and no interior pegs, 3 boundary pegs and 1 interior peg, 3 boundary pegs and 2 interior pegs, and so on.

- Copy each polygon onto geodot paper and record the number of boundary pegs, the number of interior pegs, and the area.

- Repeat the investigation for polygons with 4, 5, and 6 boundary pegs.

- Look for patterns that can help you predict the areas of new polygons.

- Organize and display your data in such a way that you can share it with the class.

The Bigger Picture

Thinking and Sharing

Call on volunteers to post solutions until several samples of each kind of polygon are on display. Have groups share their observations and any generalizations they made. Encourage the class to test the generalizations using new shapes. Also, invite groups to share their record-keeping methods with the class if they feel they had a system that helped make patterns evident.

Use prompts such as these to promote class discussion:

- Which polygons had areas that were easy to find? Which ones were more difficult? Why?

- What strategies did you use to find the areas?

- What patterns did you find in your data? Do you think the patterns will work for other polygons? How do you know?

- Did seeing patterns help you with your work? How?

- What do you think the area of a polygon with 7 boundary pegs and no interior pegs might be? Explain your prediction.

Writing

Ask children to describe how they used patterns to help them in their work on this activity.

Extending the Activity

1. Have children test their generalizations by creating polygons with more than 7 boundary pegs. Have them add the new data to their charts, and verify their generalizations.

Where's the Mathematics?

Children should find that all shapes with the same number of boundary pegs and the same number of interior pegs have the same area.

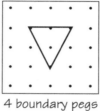
4 boundary pegs
1 interior peg
Area = 2 square units

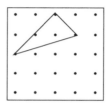
4 boundary pegs
1 interior peg
Area = 2 square units

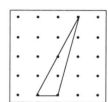
4 boundary pegs
1 interior peg
Area = 2 square units

They may also discover that when the number of boundary pegs remains constant, there is an increase of 1 square unit in area each time another interior peg is added.

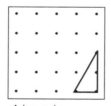
4 boundary pegs
no interior pegs
Area = 1 square unit

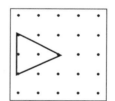
4 boundary pegs
1 interior peg
Area = 2 square units

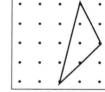
4 boundary pegs
2 interior pegs
Area = 3 square units

As children collect more and more data, they may begin to see the value of some type of organized record keeping. Such record keeping may help to make the area patterns more apparent. These patterns enable children to predict the area for the new polygons they make, and determine the area for polygons that have areas that are difficult to figure out. The tables on the following page show one way children might organize their data.

Once their data has been organized in this or some other way, children may notice that when the number of interior pegs remains constant, there is an increase of 1/2 square unit in area each time another boundary peg is added.

2. Present Pick's Theorem to the children (Area = B/2 + I - 1, where B = the number of boundary pegs, and I = the number of interior pegs). Have them verify that their results from the exploration in the activity fit the formula. Then have them test the theorem on other Geoboard polygons.

Boundary Pegs	Interior Pegs	Area in Sq. Units
3	0	½
3	1	1 ½
3	2	2 ½
3	3	3 ½
3	4	4 ½
3	5	5 ½
3	6	6 ½

Boundary Pegs	Interior Pegs	Area in Sq. Units
4	0	1
4	1	2
4	2	3
4	3	4
4	4	5
4	5	6
4	6	7

Boundary Pegs	Interior Pegs	Area in Sq. Units
5	0	1 ½
5	1	2 ½
5	2	3 ½
5	3	4 ½
5	4	5 ½
5	5	6 ½
5	6	7 ½

Boundary Pegs	Interior Pegs	Area in Sq. Units
6	0	2
6	1	3
6	2	4
6	3	5
6	4	6
6	5	7
6	6	8

Using the pattern in the first rows of the tables, children may be able to conclude that a polygon with 7 boundary pegs and no interior pegs has an area of 2½ square units. Then, by studying the patterns in the columns of the tables, children will be able to conclude that, with the addition of each interior peg, the area of a polygon with 7 boundary pegs will increase by 1 square unit.

As a follow-up for this activity, you may wish to introduce Pick's Theorem, Area = B/2 + I – 1. It states that the area of a polygon on the Geoboard can be found by dividing the number of boundary pegs (B) by 2, adding the number of interior pegs (I), and subtracting 1. Children can then use this theorem to make predictions about other Geoboard polygons without actually making them. For example, a polygon with 8 boundary pegs and 5 interior pegs would have an area of 8/2 + 5 – 1, or 8 square units.

As children try out the formula by substituting values for B and I and comparing the results with their solutions in the activity, they begin to understand that this formula is an example of how a pattern can be summarized and used to make predictions.

PEG CAPTURE

- Using a coordinate system
- Game strategies

Getting Ready

What You'll Need

Geoboards, 1 per pair

Sticky dots, 10 per pair

Square paper markers, 10 each of 2 crayon colors per pair, page 95

Overhead Geoboard and/or geodot paper transparency (optional)

Overview

In this game for two players, children use a coordinate system to name and locate Geoboard pegs. Then they play a game in which the object is to get four markers lined up horizontally, vertically, or diagonally. In this activity, children have the opportunity to:

◆ use ordered pairs to describe location

◆ use strategic thinking

The Activity

Before introducing the activity, number the rows and columns of pegs on your Geoboard using sticky dots as shown. Instead of sticky dots, you may want to use a coordinate Geoboard mat.

You may want to play a game of Peg Capture with children before they begin the On Their Own.

Introducing

- ◆ Display a Geoboard with rows and columns marked as shown. Explain that the location of every peg is indicated by two numbers, or an ordered pair of numbers.

- ◆ Write (2, 3) on the chalkboard and press a marker onto the corresponding peg.

- ◆ Do the same for (4, 0).

- ◆ Ask children to explain how you knew where to put the markers.

- ◆ Establish that, starting with the peg at (0, 0), the first number of an ordered pair tells how many pegs to count across. The second number tells how many pegs to count upward. Point out that a zero in an ordered pair means "no movement."

On Their Own

Play *Peg Capture!*

Here are the rules.

1. This is a game for 2 players. The object of the game is to get 4 markers in a row horizontally, vertically, or diagonally.

2. Players use a Geoboard and sticky dots to make a game board as shown.

3. Each player chooses a color of square paper markers. Players decide who will go first.

4. Players, in turn, call out an ordered pair of numbers, then "capture" the matching peg by pressing a marker onto it.

5. If a player thinks the other player made a mistake in placing a marker, he or she may challenge the other player's move. Together the players check the move. Whoever was wrong loses a turn.

6. Play continues until someone captures four pegs in a row. If neither player can get four in a row, the game is a draw.

- Play several games of *Peg Capture*.
- Be ready to talk about good moves and bad moves.

The Bigger Picture

Thinking and Sharing

Invite children to talk about their games and to describe some of the thinking they did.

Use prompts like these to promote class discussion:

- Is there a best first move? If so, what is it?
- Do you have any other favorite moves? What are they? Are they good moves?
- Did you make any moves you wanted to take back? Why?
- Did you have a moment of surprise during the game? Try to describe that moment.
- Did anyone develop a strategy that will always work? Tell about it.
- What kinds of things did you think about when you planned your moves? How did you decide which pegs to capture?

Writing

Have children describe how to use an ordered pair to locate pegs on the Geoboard.

1. Have children use the same set of rules to play the game *Make a Square* in which they try to capture four pegs that form the corners of a square. Variations of this could be *Make a Rectangle, Make a Right Triangle, Make a Parallelogram*, and so forth.

Teacher Talk

Where's the Mathematics?

Peg Capture gives children experience in working with one of the simplest, yet most powerful, ideas in all mathematics—coordinate graphing. This idea makes it possible to represent an algebraic concept geometrically. A simplified description of coordinate graphing is this: If a pair of perpendicular lines are imposed on a plane, the location of any point in the plane can be identified by its distance from each of the two perpendicular lines.

As they play *Peg Capture*, children can gain an appreciation of the value of using ordered pairs of numbers to identify locations. Although the pegs could be labeled in some other way, such as by letters or by numbers from 1 to 25, a system of ordered pairs of numbers has the beauty of efficiency and economy. This system is also easily expanded to a grid of any size.

If children are new to this concept of coordinate graphing, they may experience some initial difficulty in using ordered pairs to name locations.

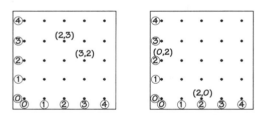

For example, they may reverse the order of the numbers or forget that the counting of the pegs in the rows and columns begins with 0 and not 1. Children may also have difficulty naming pegs where one of the coordinates is 0. Through practice, their ability to properly identify locations improves. In fact, children may start to see patterns in the numbers of the ordered pairs and in the location of corresponding pegs. For example, they may come to realize that all ordered pairs with the same first coordinate name pegs in the

2. Have children play several games of each of two other forms of *Peg Capture*—one in which the object is to place 3 markers in a row and the other in which the object is to place 5 markers in a row. Then ask them to compare the strategies for games involving 3, 4, and 5 markers in a row.

same column. Likewise, ordered pairs with the same second coordinate name pegs in the same row.

Ordered pairs
in a column
have the
same first
coordinate.

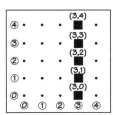

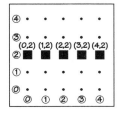

Ordered pairs
in a row have
the same
second
coordinate.

Children may make the connection that strategies for winning *Peg Capture* are similar to those for winning in the game of *Tic-Tac-Toe*. The main differences are that, in *Peg Capture*, the playing area is not confined to a three-by-three grid and that it is possible to win without having the line of markers go all the way across the game board.

1st move

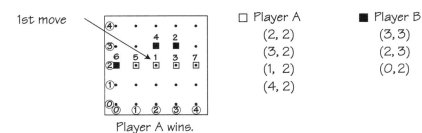

Player A wins.

□ Player A	■ Player B
(2, 2)	(3, 3)
(3, 2)	(2, 3)
(1, 2)	(0, 2)
(4, 2)	

As children look for winning strategies, they may come to realize that it is helpful to capture pegs near the center of the board early in the game. This strategy gives children opportunities to pursue moves in many directions while preventing opponents from easily blocking them. They may also discover that there is no particular advantage to going first or second.

POSSIBLE/ IMPOSSIBLE

Getting Ready

What You'll Need

Geoboards, 1 per child

Rubber bands

Geodot paper, pages 90–91

Overhead Geoboard and/or geodot paper transparency (optional)

Overview

Children try to make Geoboard polygons that fit given descriptions. In this activity, children have the opportunity to:

◆ explore attributes of different polygons

◆ use mathematical reasoning to determine whether or not it is possible to make a shape having a particular set of attributes

◆ use geometric language to describe polygons and their attributes

The Activity

You may want to review these terms before doing the lesson: obtuse angle, right angle, congruent angles, congruent sides, parallel sides, isosceles triangle, hexagon, convex polygon, *and* concave polygon.

Introducing

◆ Ask children to make a triangle that has 4 interior pegs on their Geoboards.

◆ Have children hold up their Geoboards. Ask them to discuss how their triangles are alike and how they are different.

On Their Own

What kinds of shapes can you make on a Geoboard?

- Work with a group to decide if it is possible or impossible to make a Geoboard shape that fits each of the descriptions below.

  - If it is possible to make a shape, record it on geodot paper. Then see if you can find and record more shapes that fit that description.

  - If it is impossible to make a shape, be ready to explain why.

Possible or Impossible?

1. A triangle with 5 interior pegs
2. A triangle with 6 interior pegs
3. A triangle with 7 interior pegs
4. An isosceles triangle with one obtuse angle
5. An isosceles triangle with one right angle
6. An isosceles triangle with no angles congruent
7. A square with sides longer than 2 units but shorter than 3 units
8. A square with an area of 6 square units
9. A hexagon with no parallel sides
10. A hexagon with 3 parallel sides
11. A hexagon with no congruent sides
12. A hexagon with all sides congruent

The Bigger Picture

Thinking and Sharing

Create 12 columns with headings corresponding to each description. Have volunteers post their solutions in the appropriate columns. For each description that they determined to be "impossible to make," have children discuss why they reached that decision. If disagreements occur, allow time for children to work together to prove or disprove their points.

Use prompts like these to promote class discussion:

- What discoveries did you make while searching for solutions?
- Which descriptions were the easiest to make shapes for? Which were the most difficult? Why?
- How did you decide when it was impossible to find a solution?
- Do you think that some of the shapes that you labeled "impossible to make" would be possible to draw on plain paper? Explain.

Writing

Ask children to choose some of the "impossible" descriptions and tell how to change them in order to make them "possible."

Where's the Mathematics?

The first six descriptions focus on triangles and some of their Geoboard properties. Here are "possible" triangles for the first two. Children's triangles may be congruent to these but in different orientations.

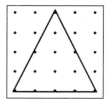

a triangle with
5 interior pegs

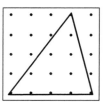

a triangle with
6 interior pegs

Some children may use trial and error to find out that it is impossible to make a triangle with 7 interior pegs (third description). Others may study the results for the first two statements and realize the impossibility of locating the third vertex so that the triangle would cover any more pegs. Thus, they come to the conclusion that the maximum number of interior pegs for a Geoboard triangle is 6.

Below are some of the possible triangles for the fourth and fifth descriptions. When children compare all their isosceles triangles, they may see that isosceles triangles, in addition to having at least two sides that are congruent, always have at least two acute angles that are congruent. This fact makes the sixth description, isosceles triangle with no angles congruent, impossible.

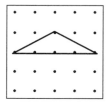

an isosceles triangle
with 1 obtuse angle

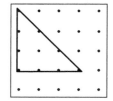

an isosceles triangle
with 1 right angle

sides longer
than 2
units, but
shorter
than 3 units

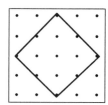

To find a square with sides longer than 2 units but shorter than 3 units, children have to realize that the diagonal distance between two pegs is greater than the horizontal or vertical distance between two pegs. Children who are not sure how to compare such distances may want to use rulers.

It is impossible to make a Geoboard square with an area of 6 square units. One way children may convince themselves of this is to make a rectangle

Extending the Activity

Have children work with their groups to write descriptions of polygons (some possible, some impossible) using other attributes such as symmetry, angle size, and area measure. Have them exchange lists with other groups, and find out which are possible.

with an area of 6 square units and try to adjust the side lengths to form a square with the same area.

When children attempt to make hexagons with sides that are parallel, they may produce shapes that are concave, or dented, such as the ones below. In the middle hexagon, the parallel sides are easily identifiable because they are built along vertical lines of pegs. When the parallel sides are not built along vertical or horizontal lines of pegs, children may need ways to convince themselves that the sides are really parallel. One justification might be that if the sides were extended to form lines, they would never meet. Another might be that the parallel sides rise or fall at the same rate. For example, in the third hexagon below, each of the three parallel sides is formed by starting at one peg and then moving 2 pegs to the right and 1 peg upward.

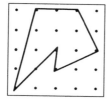

a hexagon with
no parallel sides

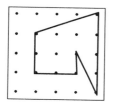

a hexagon with
3 parallel sides

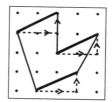

a hexagon with
3 parallel sides

Children may be surprised to see that though the eleventh description is possible, the twelfth is impossible.

a hexagon with no
congruent sides

the diagonal distance between
pegs is not the same as the
horizontal distance between pegs

Children should realize that some shapes that are impossible to make on the Geoboard can be drawn on plain paper. For example, many different-sized squares with sides between 2 and 3 units can be drawn on paper, as can a hexagon with all congruent sides. Children's explanations as to why certain shapes cannot be made on the Geoboard may reflect the depth of their understanding about geometric concepts and the limitations of the Geoboard.

SHAPE RIDDLES

- Polygons
- Spatial visualization
- Properties of geometric figures

Getting Ready

What You'll Need

Geoboards, 1 per child

Rubber bands

Geodot paper, page 90

Overhead Geoboard and/or geodot paper transparency (optional)

Overview

Children solve riddles by making Geoboard polygons that fit given sets of clues. In this activity, children have the opportunity to:

- identify distinguishing attributes that differentiate polygons
- apply logical reasoning to find solutions that fit a set of clues
- use geometric language to describe properties of polygons

Introductory Riddle

It is a quadrilateral.

Its angles are all congruent.

Its length is twice its width.

The Activity

Introducing

- Ask children to construct any 4-sided figure, or quadrilateral, on their Geoboards. Then give them this riddle.

> It is a quadrilateral.
> Its angles are all the same size, or congruent.
> Its length is twice its width.

- Ask children to decide whether or not their quadrilaterals fit the clues in the riddle. Have volunteers explain their decisions.

- Discuss these three possible solutions, and have children explain why there are only three solutions.

On Their Own

Can you solve these Geoboard riddles by making shapes that fit the clues?

Riddle 1

It has 3 sides.
Each side is a different length.
It has one interior peg.
It has no right angles.

Riddle 2

It has 4 sides.
It has only 1 pair of parallel sides.
No sides are the same length, or congruent.

Riddle 3

It has 6 sides.
It has an area of 5 square units.
It has 2 right angles.

- Work with a group to find several possible solutions for each riddle.
- Record your solutions on geodot paper.
- Be ready to explain how you found your solutions.

The Bigger Picture

Thinking and Sharing

Have groups take turns presenting solutions for each of the riddles. Write the clues for each riddle on a different section of the chalkboard. Post the solutions for each riddle under its clues. Encourage children to discuss how the solutions are alike and how they are different.

Use prompts such as these to promote class discussion:

- How did you go about solving the riddles?
- Which kinds of clues were easiest to follow? Which were more difficult? Why?
- What mathematical names could you give the shapes you have made?
- For each riddle, how might you add a clue (or clues) that would lead to only one possible solution?

You may want to save the postings of children's solutions and encourage them to add any new solutions they find over the next few days.

Writing

Have children make a list of words that are the most helpful in the clues in this activity. Have them explain why they are good "clue words."

Extending the Activity

Have children work in pairs or small groups to write their own riddles for other groups to solve. Ask children to vary the kinds of riddles that they write. For example, children could write riddles that have several solutions, just one solution, or no solutions.

Where's the Mathematics?

Children develop their logical reasoning ability as they experiment to find polygons that fit the clues in the riddles. Children also become more familiar with the properties of polygons, as well as with the geometric language that is used to describe these properties.

The following drawings show three possible solutions for each riddle and the mathematical terms that describe the solutions. Children, however, will probably explain these solutions in their own terms. For example, instead of scalene they may say "no sides that are the same."

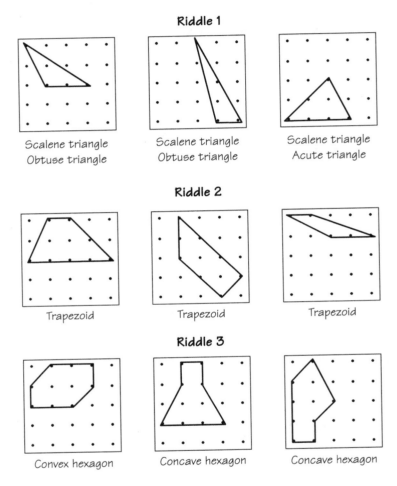

Riddle 1

Scalene triangle
Obtuse triangle

Scalene triangle
Obtuse triangle

Scalene triangle
Acute triangle

Riddle 2

Trapezoid

Trapezoid

Trapezoid

Riddle 3

Convex hexagon

Concave hexagon

Concave hexagon

Children may go about solving the riddles in different ways. Some children may form a shape that fits the first clue, and then adjust the shape as they read each successive clue. For example, for Riddle 1:

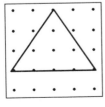
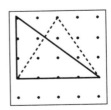

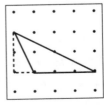

3 sides

No congruent sides

1 interior peg

No right angles

Other children may read the whole riddle, reforming a shape in their minds until they think it fits all the clues. Then they make the shape on their Geoboard and check it against the clues.

Some children may use the process of elimination to solve the riddles. For example, in the riddle in the *Introducing*, the first two clues eliminate all shapes except squares and rectangles. The third clue eliminates the squares and narrows down the possible rectangles to those that have lengths that are twice their widths. Although these rectangles can be positioned differently on the Geoboard, they are all slides, flips, or turns of only three unique rectangles. Thus, through experimentation, children find that there are only three rectangles on the Geoboard that are solutions to this riddle.

When adding clues to a riddle so that it will produce a unique solution, children may focus on one particular solution and look for ways to eliminate all the other solutions. For example, in order to make the shape below the unique solution for Riddle 1, children would have to add clues such as the following:

Additional Clues:
One side is 3 units long.
It has an obtuse angle.

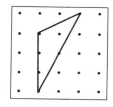

These additional clues will make this shape the unique solution for Riddle 2.

Additional Clues:
The shorter of the parallel sides is
    3 units long.
The shortest side is 2 units long.

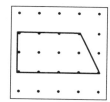

These additional clues will make this shape the unique solution for Riddle 3.

Additional Clues:
There are 3 pairs of parallel sides.
One pair of parallel sides are each
    2 units long.
One pair of parallel sides are each
    1 unit long.

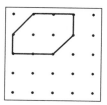

SQUARE SEARCH

Getting Ready

What You'll Need

Geoboards, 1 per child

Rubber bands

Geodot paper, pages 90–91 and 95

Geodot writing paper, page 96

Overhead Geoboard and/or geodot paper transparency (optional)

Overview

Children search for all the different-sized squares that can be made on the Geoboard. They then find the area of each of their squares. In this activity, children have the opportunity to:

♦ use a variety of methods to find area

♦ use logical reasoning to find all possibilities

The Activity

You may want to provide some experience with finding area on the Geoboard before doing this lesson. See introductory material.

Introducing

♦ Ask children to brainstorm a list of things they know about squares.
For example: four equal sides
four right angles
opposite sides parallel
no acute or obtuse angles
four lines of symmetry
quarter-turn symmetry
half-turn symmetry

♦ Then ask children to make a square on their Geoboards.

♦ Have the class check the squares against the attributes on their list.

On Their Own

> ## How many different-sized squares can you make on a Geoboard?
>
> - Work with your group to make as many different-sized squares as you can.
> - Find the area of each square you make.
> - Record each square on geodot paper and label its area.
> - Compare your recorded squares to make sure they are all different sizes.
> - Be ready to explain how you know you have found all the possible solutions.

The Bigger Picture

Thinking and Sharing

Have groups take turns showing one of their squares and telling how they found its area. Post each of the possible squares and label its area.

Use prompts such as these to promote class discussion:

- How are the squares you found different from each other?
- How did you decide you had found all the possible squares? How could you convince someone else of this?
- How did you find the areas of the squares? Are there other ways to find the area? What are they?
- Which areas were easy to find? Which were more difficult? Why?
- What else did you discover about squares?

Drawing and Writing

Ask children to explain how to find the area of a square whose sides are not parallel to the edges of the Geoboard. Have them draw the square to illustrate their explanation.

Extending the Activity

1. Have children find all the different-sized rectangles that can be made on a Geoboard.
2. Have children find all the different-sized right triangles that can be made on a Geoboard.

Where's the Mathematics?

There are 8 different squares in all. The squares with areas of 1, 4, 9, and 16 square units will probably be the most obvious for children to find since they can count the unit squares that fill these squares.

1 square unit

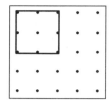

4 square units

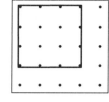

9 square units

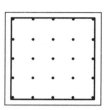

16 square units

Some children may already know the area formula and might find the area by multiplying the length of one side by the length of another. You may want to have all the children verify this method by having them test it on the four squares shown above. Some children may point out that since all the sides of a square have the same length, they can find the areas by multiplying the length of one side by itself.

Squares with areas of 2, 5, 8, and 10 square units are shown below. To discover these squares, children must recognize that squares do not necessarily have to have sides that are parallel to the edges of the Geoboard. Finding the areas of these squares may prove to be somewhat challenging for some children.

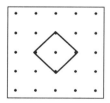

2 square units

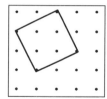

5 square units

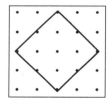

8 square units

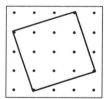

10 square units

There are several ways children might figure the area of these squares. Some children may divide their squares into parts, figure the areas of the separate parts, and then add these areas together. For example, the square with an area of 2 square units may be divided into 4 congruent triangles, each with an area of 1/2 square unit, resulting in a total area of 2 square units.

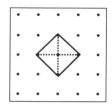

area = ½ + ½ + ½ + ½
     = 2 square units

Other children may enclose one of these squares with a larger square that has sides parallel to the edges of the Geoboard, figure the area of the larger square, and subtract the areas of the parts of the larger square that do not lie within the smaller square. For example, the larger square enclosing the square with area 2 square units has an area of 4 square units. When the areas of the parts not enclosed by the smaller square (the triangular corners with area of 1/2 square unit each) are subtracted, the area remaining (that of the smaller square) is 2 square units.

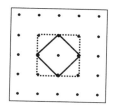

$$\text{area} = 4 - \tfrac{1}{2} - \tfrac{1}{2} - \tfrac{1}{2} - \tfrac{1}{2}$$
$$= 2 \text{ square units}$$

The same method can be used to find the area of the tilted square shown below. The larger square enclosing this square has an area of 16 square units. There are four triangular regions that are not enclosed by the tilted square. Each of these triangular regions has an area that is one-half of 3 square units, or $1\tfrac{1}{2}$ square units.

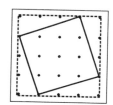

$$\text{area} = 16 - 1\tfrac{1}{2} - 1\tfrac{1}{2} - 1\tfrac{1}{2} - 1\tfrac{1}{2}$$
$$= 10 \text{ square units}$$

Children may describe other methods for finding area. Some may be combinations of the techniques described, while others may be totally different procedures that children found useful. Encourage them to describe their strategies, and to demonstrate how they used them to find the areas of their squares.

Children may also offer a variety of arguments to explain how they know they have found all the squares. Their explanations may provide insight into their understanding of the geometric properties of squares.

SQUARES AROUND A TRIANGLE

- **Properties of right triangles**
- **Area**

Getting Ready

What You'll Need

Geoboards, 1 per child

Rubber bands

Dot paper, page 92

Overhead Geoboard and/or dot paper transparency (optional)

Overview

Children examine squares built on the sides of right triangles made on a Geoboard. They then look for a relationship among the areas of the squares. In this activity, children have the opportunity to:

- ◆ apply strategies for finding areas
- ◆ explore relationships among the sides of right triangles
- ◆ generalize from recorded data

The Activity

You may want to provide some experiences with finding area on the Geoboard before doing this lesson. See introductory material.

Introducing

- ◆ Have children copy this shape on their Geoboards.

- ◆ Ask children to make a square on each side of the shape so that one side of each new square is also a side of the original shape.

- ◆ Have children compare results and verify that they have made a square on each side.

On Their Own

How are the squares on the sides of a Geoboard right triangle related?

- Work with a group. Each of you make a different-sized right triangle on your Geoboard.

- Record your triangle toward the middle of a piece of dot paper.

- Build a square on each side of your triangle. Be sure that each complete side of your triangle is also a complete side of a square. You may want to use a ruler to help you make the sides of your squares.

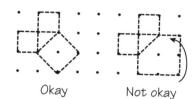

Okay   Not okay

- Find and record the area of each square.

- Check each other's work.

- Look for relationships among the areas of the 3 squares surrounding each triangle.

The Bigger Picture

Thinking and Sharing

Invite children to share their observations about the areas of the three squares they made on a triangle. Encourage children to help each other to find the areas of any squares they had difficulty working with.

Use prompts like these to promote class discussion:

- How did you determine the areas of the squares? Are there other ways to find the areas?

- What patterns did you discover?

- Do you think you would find this pattern in all right triangles? Why?

- What generalization can you make about the areas of the three squares built on the sides of a right triangle?

Extending the Activity

1. Have the children repeat the activity using triangles in which all three angles are acute. (Children should find that the area of the square on the longest side will be less than the sum of the areas of the two smaller squares.)

2. Have children also repeat the activity using triangles containing one obtuse angle. (Children should find that the area of the square on the longest side will be greater than the sum of the areas of the two smaller squares.)

Where's the Mathematics?

In examining the areas of the squares surrounding each right triangle, children notice that the sum of the areas of the squares on the two shorter sides of the triangle is equal to the area of the square on the longest side of the triangle. For any right triangle, where a and b are the lengths of the legs and c is the length of the hypotenuse, this relationship, known as the Pythagorean Theorem, can be stated algebraically as $a^2 + b^2 = c^2$.

Children may use different strategies to find the areas of the squares they make. For the squares that have edges parallel to the edges of the dot paper, children may count the number of unit squares contained in the squares. Some children may realize that the area of these squares can be found by multiplying the length of one side of the square by itself.

To find the areas of the squares whose sides are not parallel to the edges of the dot paper, children may use partitioning techniques to divide the squares into shapes whose areas may be easier to find.

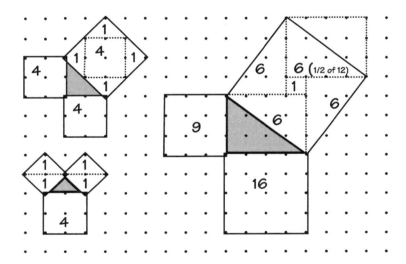

Children may also find the areas of squares by enclosing them inside squares whose sides are parallel to the edges of the dot paper. The areas of these "enclosing squares" can then be determined (by counting unit squares or by squaring the length of a side). Then the areas of the four triangular regions formed outside the original square can be subtracted from the area of the enclosing square.

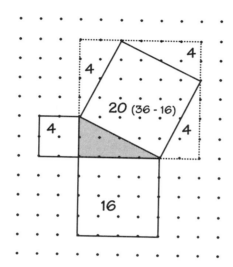

This activity allows children to discover geometric relationships that prepare them for their eventual work with irrational numbers—in particular, finding square roots.

TRIANGLE SEARCH

- Area
- Properties of triangles
- Congruence

Getting Ready

What You'll Need

Geoboards, 1 per child

Rubber bands

Geodot paper, pages 90–91

Overhead Geoboard and/or geodot paper transparency (optional)

Overview

On their Geoboards, children try to make different triangles having the same area. In this activity, children have the opportunity to:

- ◆ develop strategies for finding area
- ◆ use logical reasoning to search for area patterns
- ◆ learn that triangles with the same area may be non-congruent

The Activity

You may want to provide some experiences with finding area on the Geoboard before doing this lesson. See introductory material.

Introducing

- ◆ Display these Geoboard shapes. Ask children to tell how the shapes are alike and how they are different.

- ◆ Establish that the shapes are alike in that they are all triangles and that each triangle has an area of 2 square units. They are different in that each has a different shape; that is, there are no two that are congruent.

On Their Own

> *How many different triangles with the same area can you make on a Geoboard?*
>
> - Work with a group. Each of you should use 1 rubber band to make a Geoboard triangle that is different from everyone else's. Record your triangles on geodot paper and label the areas.
>
> - Continue to make and record triangles until you have made one for each of the possible areas that a Geoboard triangle can have.
>
> - Then work together to create and record as many different triangles as you can for each possible area.
>
> - Be ready to explain how you know you have found all the possible triangles for each area.

The Bigger Picture

Thinking and Sharing

Call on an volunteer to name the smallest area for a Geoboard triangle. Invite children to post the different triangles they found that had this area. Then have another volunteer give the next possible area. Ask children to post the different triangles with this area. Continue this process until there are examples posted for each possible area.

Use prompts like these to promote class discussion:

- Were the areas of some triangles easier to figure out than others? Which ones? Which areas were more difficult to find?

- How did you find the area of your triangles? Are there other ways to do this? If so, what are they?

- How did you decide you had found all the possible triangles? How could you convince someone else of this?

- Did you see any patterns in the data you collected? Did the patterns help you discover anything?

- What else did you discover about triangles?

Writing

Ask children to describe their strategy or strategies for finding new triangles that had the same areas as triangles they had already found.

Extending the Activity

Have children reproduce the triangles they made on large geodot paper and cut them out. Then have them find different ways to sort the triangles, for example, by side length or by angle measure.

Where's the Mathematics?

As children work through this activity, they discover that it is possible to make triangles with 16 different areas. One triangle of each area is shown below.

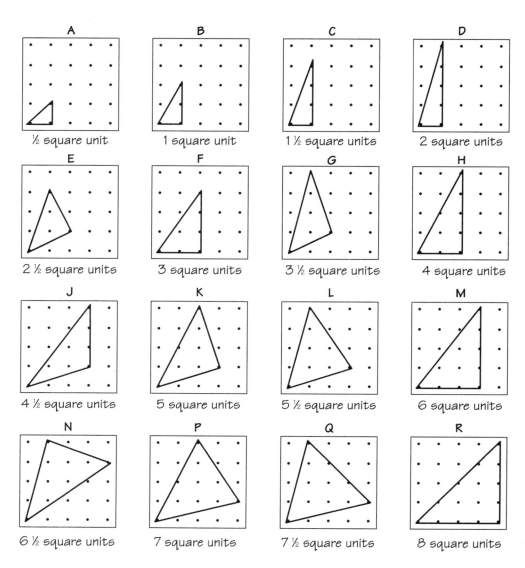

A	B	C	D
½ square unit	1 square unit	1 ½ square units	2 square units
E	**F**	**G**	**H**
2 ½ square units	3 square units	3 ½ square units	4 square units
J	**K**	**L**	**M**
4 ½ square units	5 square units	5 ½ square units	6 square units
N	**P**	**Q**	**R**
6 ½ square units	7 square units	7 ½ square units	8 square units

Children use a variety of strategies for finding the possible areas for Geoboard triangles. Some children may start by focusing on the right triangles that have two sides that are parallel to the edges of the Geoboard. This will lead to solutions like A, B, C, D, F, H, M, and R shown above. Children can find the area of each of these triangles, 1/2, 1, 1½, 2, 3, 4, 6, and 8 square units respectively, by finding the area of the surrounding rectangle and halving it.

Children need different strategies to find triangles with areas of 2½, 3½, 4½, 5, 5½, 6½, 7, and 7½ square units. These triangles have only one side or no sides that are parallel to a Geoboard edge.

When a triangle has one side parallel to the Geoboard edge, different triangles with the same area can be found by moving the opposite vertex along the row (or column) of pegs that is parallel to that side.

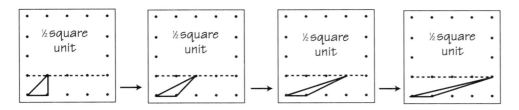

Children who are familiar with the formula for finding the area of a triangle (Area = 1/2 • base • height) may form triangles that have one or two sides parallel to an edge of their Geoboards and then apply the formula. For example:

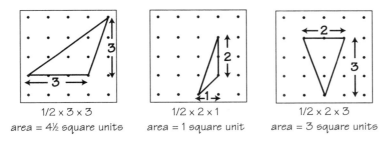

| 1/2 x 3 x 3 | 1/2 x 2 x 1 | 1/2 x 2 x 3 |
| area = 4½ square units | area = 1 square unit | area = 3 square units |

When a triangle has no sides parallel to a Geoboard edge, it is more difficult to find different triangles with the same area. Most children will use a trial and error approach. Encourage them to share how they found the different triangles and the strategies they used to find their areas.

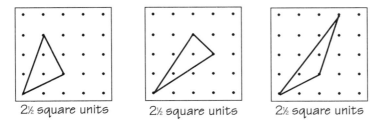

| 2½ square units | 2½ square units | 2½ square units |

Children may recognize a pattern and conclude that they should have triangles that have areas that range from 1/2 square unit to 8 square units in increments of 1/2. This conjecture may help children to either find these triangles, or to calculate the area of triangles that they had trouble with.

WHAT'S ISOSCELES?

- **Properties of triangles**
- **Congruence**
- **Pattern recognition**

Getting Ready

What You'll Need

Circular Geoboard, 1 per child

Rubber bands

Rulers

Circular Geodot paper, page 94

Geodot writing paper, page 96

Overhead circular Geoboard and/or circular geodot paper transparency (optional)

Overview

Children try to make all the possible isosceles triangles that can be made on a circular Geoboard and then look for patterns. In this activity, children have the opportunity to:

- ◆ use deductive reasoning to find angle measure
- ◆ discover that in a triangle the congruent angles are located opposite the congruent sides
- ◆ learn that congruent chords intercept congruent arcs

The Activity

Before children work on the activity, you may want to introduce the lesson Inscribed Triangles (page 50) in which they discover that the measure of an inscribed angle is one-half the measure of its intercepted arc.

Introducing

- ◆ Show children a circular Geoboard and ask them to imagine that it is a clock. Tell them that the circle around the clockface measures 360°. Use your finger to trace the arc from the 12 peg to the 1 peg. Ask children how many degrees are in this arc and how they know. Establish that the arc connecting consecutive pegs is 1/12 of the circle, or 30°.

- ◆ Now show children this circular Geoboard. Tell them that this is a *central angle* because it opens out from, or has its vertex on, the center peg of the circle.

intercepted arc

- ◆ Ask children what the measure of this central angle is and how they think it is related to the arc it intercepts. Establish that the angle is 90°, and since the arc went from the 12 peg to the 3 peg it was 90° also.

- ◆ Establish that the number of degrees in a central angle is equal to the number of degrees in the arc it intercepts.

On Their Own

How many **different isosceles triangles** can you make on a circular Geoboard?

- Work with a partner to create different isosceles triangles. An isosceles has at least 2 equal sides. The vertices of the triangles can be at the center peg and any 2 pegs on the circle, or they can be at 3 pegs on the circle.

- Find the measure of each angle of the triangles. Here's how. Find the measure of the arc that the sides of the angle intercept:

  central angle   inscribed angle

  - Each arc from peg to peg around the circle measures 30°.
  - A central angle equals that arc.
  - An inscribed angle is ½ of that arc.

- Record each triangle and its angle measurements on circular geodot paper.

- Find as many different isosceles triangles as you can.

- Be prepared to discuss what all of your triangles have in common.

The Bigger Picture

Thinking and Sharing

Ask volunteers, one by one, to create one of the triangles they found on their Geoboard, put the Geoboard on the chalk tray, and write the angle measurements above it. Continue until children feel that every possible isosceles triangle is displayed.

Use prompts like these to promote class discussion:

- How many triangles did you find?
- How did you know that the sides of the triangle were congruent?
- What do all your triangles have in common?
- What are the properties of an isosceles triangle?
- Is an equilateral triangle also an isosceles triangle? Explain.
- If you know which sides are congruent, how can you tell which angles are congruent?
- Do you notice any other patterns? What are they?

Writing

Have children draw a sketch of an isosceles triangle and write its definition so that a friend can read it and understand what makes an isosceles triangle special.

Extending the Activity

1. Have children sort the triangles they found in this lesson according to these categories: acute isosceles triangles, right isosceles triangles, and obtuse isosceles triangles.

Teacher Talk

Where's the Mathematics?

Many children in this age group know that an isosceles triangle has two congruent sides. This activity provides them with an opportunity to extend their list of attributes of an isosceles triangle to include two congruent angles and learn that those congruent angles are located opposite the congruent sides. They also work extensively with central and inscribed angles of a circle. The ten possible isosceles triangles and their angle measures are shown below:

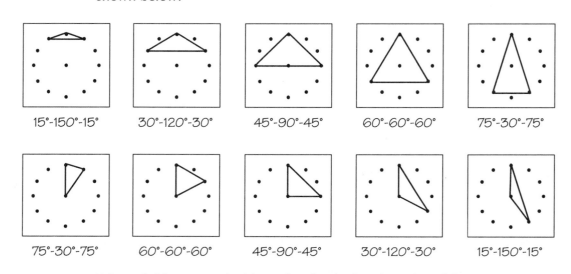

| 15°-150°-15° | 30°-120°-30° | 45°-90°-45° | 60°-60°-60° | 75°-30°-75° |

| 75°-30°-75° | 60°-60°-60° | 45°-90°-45° | 30°-120°-30° | 15°-150°-15° |

When children are asked how they knew that the sides of the triangle were congruent, some may rely on intuition and say that "they looked equal." Others may observe that they counted pegs or used the intercepted arc. For example, in this equilateral triangle, once the rubber band is placed at the 12 peg, the next vertex is located 4 pegs away at the 4 peg and the third vertex is 4 pegs beyond that at the 8 peg. Dividing the circle into equal arcs makes the sides of the triangles equal, too. Students will see this idea resurface in high school geometry class as the theorem "congruent chords intercept congruent arcs." Chords refer to line segments that connect two points on a circle.

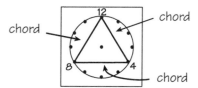

For the isosceles triangles formed using the center point of the circle, the congruent sides will be the radii of the circle. Since the definition of a circle

2. Ask children to find all the quadrilaterals on the circular Geoboard that have at least two congruent sides. Have them measure the angles and look for patterns.

---

is "the set of all points in a plane equidistant from a given point," all of the radii of the circle must be congruent.

Some children will question whether an equilateral triangle is an isosceles triangle. An equilateral triangle fits the definition of an isosceles triangle in that it has *at least two* congruent sides. It may help to draw the analogy that a square is a special example of a rectangle, just as an equilateral triangle is a special example of an isosceles triangle.

Some children may discuss the patterns in angle size that they see. The size of the inscribed angles increase in increments of 15° while the central angles increase in increments of 30°. They may observe that it would not be possible to represent an angle of 25°, for instance, on a geoboard because 25 is not a multiple of 15.

As children look at the triangles and their measurements, they will probably notice that two congruent angles are always located opposite the two congruent sides of the triangle as shown on the right.

congruent angles
opposite
congruent sides

Some children will find all of the inscribed angle measurements by relying on the fact that an inscribed angle measures one-half of its intercepted arc. Some children may have to put additional rubber bands on the Geoboard to find where the intercepted arcs are located when the center of the circle is one of the vertices of the triangle. For example, the additional rubber bands pictured on the Geoboard below right will help children find the intercepted arc for the angle whose vertex is located at the 7 peg.

Other children who know that the sum of the angles of a triangle is 180° will use arithmetic to find the missing angles. In the triangle above, they will figure that the central angle is 90° because it has the same number of degrees as its intercepted arc. Since the other two angles are opposite the congruent sides, they must be congruent and have a sum that is 180 – 90, or 90°. So, each angle has 45°.

Children are likely to notice that there are five pairs of isosceles triangles that have the same angle measurements but different side lengths. These pairs of triangles are called *similar triangles*.

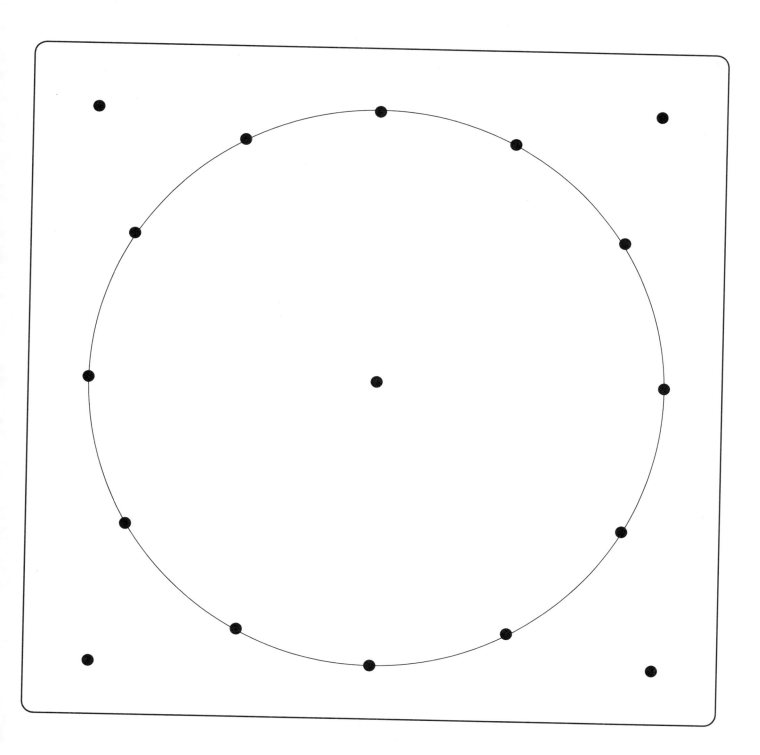

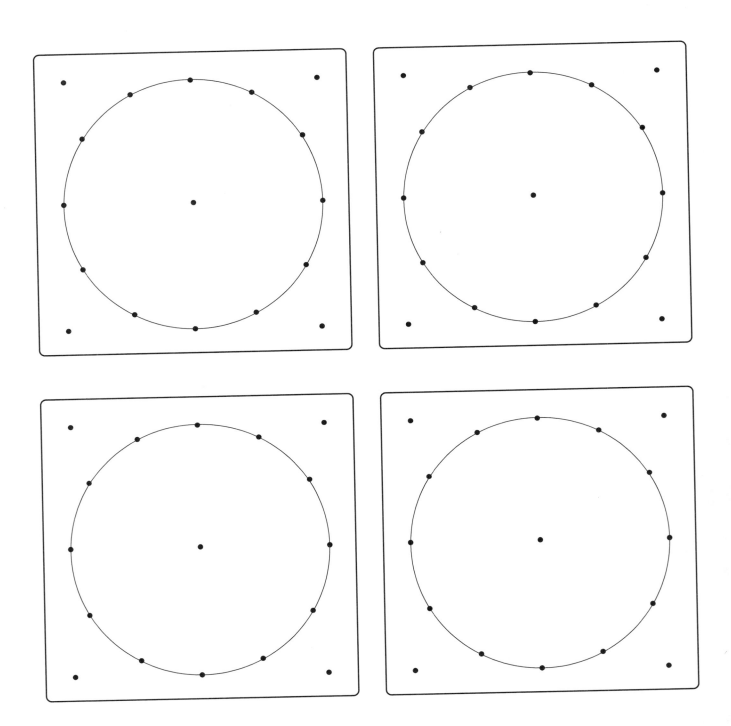

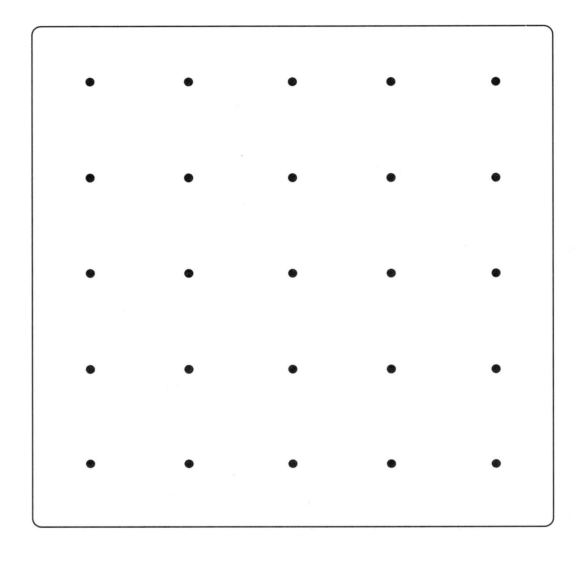